a d v a n c e   r e v i e w s

"Wake Up Inspired delivers on its promise. For those who are ready to live more deeply, freely, and creatively – Marian Baker is a worthy guide. Her new book blends skillful teaching and practical exercises into a life-changing recipe that will nourish your soul. Keep it by your bedside. Take it on your next business trip. You will find powerful truths distilled into forms that you can use to wake up your life – starting today."

> Eric Klein, Author of *You are the Leader You've Been Waiting For* and *Awakening Corporate Soul*

"Finally a writer that 'gets it.' By reading this book I felt it was speaking about my personal life. The lack of joy in today's world is overwhelming and most of us don't know an alternative. This book is profound, magnetic and amazingly simple. As the pages turned I felt myself becoming lighter with the insights Marian conveyed. A clear understanding about how to move from a non-questioning rat race life into a peaceful, exciting journey with EASE, is this book's gift to you!"

> John Vazquez, MD, Chairman, Department of Anesthesia, Mt. Sinai Medical Center

"Marian Baker's approach to creating a life where joy and holistic balance are the foundation has helped me to transform my life. Her combination of easy-to-follow exercises and funny anecdotes are insightful and practical. And, importantly, they lead to lasting change."

> Christine M. McGrath, Senior Director of New Product Development, Kraft Foods

"I LOVED this book. I could hear Marian's *wise soul* voice and spirit coming through the pages. Not only did I feel challenged, I also found myself nodding and smiling as I read. What a gift to women. I will be recommending this book to my colleagues."

Carol Wzorek, United States Department of State, Foreign Service Institute

"As a marketing professional, I have long understood that compelling brands are built one detail at a time. Marian Baker teaches that compelling lives are made the same way. I used to feel life flying by. This work has inspired me to claim the quiet moments and to connect to a higher agenda for my own life. Filled with compassion and well-timed zingers, Marian's wisdom and merry laughter can be felt in the pages of this book."

Kelly Smith, Vice President, Corporate Marketing

"Wake Up Inspired is a guide to conscious living with passion and purpose. It is a gift to readers – to notice their choices, celebrate their life and focus on the possibilities that create the future. Read this witty, compelling and practical book to raise the joyful vibration of your life!"

Marlene Bolster, AVP/Associate Administrator, Inova Fair Oaks Hospital

"This book immediately grabs your attention with the words, "*What are you living for?*" From that moment, you will be taken on a journey you will remember forever. Marian Baker is a brilliant coach, inspiring speaker, and thank goodness she is now sharing her thought-provoking and witty insights with the public. She balances the spiritual side of "waking up inspired," with a specific, step-by-step roadmap to living a deeply rewarding life. I am excited that you, fellow reader and traveler, now get to benefit from her wisdom in this incredible book."

Michael Charest, President, Business Growth Solutions and author of *From Grunt to Greatness!*

"This book helps readers capture the essence of life's experiences such that we can laugh at ourselves, learn something and move on toward more rewarding lives. Her passion in writing as in coaching is to encourage the practice of "hitting the pause button" to reflect and make optimal choices. Her writing style has the tell-on-herself approach of Anne Lamont and the memorable nature of a favorite childhood jingle that stays in your head. Without a hint of preachiness she is committed to inspiring all of us to wake up and live fully."

> Karen Radtke, Certified Executive Coach and
> Organizational Consultant, Beacon Street

"Marian's coaching has a huge impact, and this book will be an inspiration to professionals who are looking for higher fulfillment in their lives and improved bottom lines in their businesses."

> Jim Merrell, President, Ross-Merrell Associates

"Even when you think you've got your life 'knocked', something happens!   It can be a great something or a not so great something, but in either case you need someone's ear. Someone who asks unbelievable questions that go beyond the surface and take you to places you've never dreamed you could go. You need someone who supports you, and keeps you on your true path, not just the one that goes to grandma's house! Read a chapter or two of Wake up Inspired.   Then you'll know why Marian Baker herself and her book is the 'ear' that really hears you!"

> Betsy Jacobson, Change Management Consultant and
> Executive Coach, Betsy Jacobson and Associates

wake up
INSPIRED

Fuel Healthier Success
and Love the Life
You're Meant to Lead

Marian Baker, CPCC, MCC

NEW STORY PRESS

Wake Up INSPIRED: Fuel Healthier Success and Love the Life You're Meant to Lead By Marian Baker, CPCC, MCC

ISBN: 0-9779059-2-6
ISBN 13: 9780977905928

Library of Congress Control Number: 2006924853

Excerpt from "Touch Me" from Passing Through: The Later Poems by Stanley Kunitz, W.W. Norton, 1995. Reprinted by permission.

PLEASE NOTE:
Client examples in this book were inspired by real life experiences. Names and details have been changed to honor their privacy.

Cover Design: Dan Paterno (www.PaternoGroup.com)
Book Design & Consulting: Nancy Cleary (www.wymacpublishing.com)
Editor: Terry Pfister (www.terrypfister.com)
Index: Christine Frank (www.ChristineFrank.com)
Publishing Consultant: Jan King (www.eWomenPublishingNetwork.com)

New Story Press

wake up
INSPIRED

Fuel Healthier Success
and Love the Life
You're Meant to Lead

I am a little pencil
in the hand
of a writing God
who is sending a
love letter
to the world.

Mother Teresa

Dedicated to Gibby, who made her
"final transition" on Valentine's Day, 1996.
May your soul be set free and I'll see you
in my dreams, Mom.

I shut my eyes
in order to 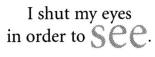.

Paul Gauguin

Do not fear mistakes…
There are none.

Miles Davis

*This is a book about changing your life.
And, you could change the life of another woman
on the other side of the world.*

While you're fueling your inspired life, how would it feel to also support life-changing opportunities for a global sister in need of our help? A portion of the proceeds of this book will be donated to Women for Women International (or other organizations inspiring and equipping women to create better lives).

About Women for Women International:

Women for Women International helps women in war-torn regions rebuild their lives by providing financial and emotional support, job skills training, rights awareness, leadership education and access to business skills, capital and markets. Through the program, women become confident, independent and productive as they embrace the importance of their roles in rebuilding their families, their communities and ultimately, their nations.

For more information or to sponsor a woman, please visit www.WomenforWomen.org.

table of contents

SECTION 1

chapter one
Waking Up to a New Story

chapter two
Having a Plan is Not the Answer

chapter three
Three Layers of Inspired Living

SECTION 2

chapter four
Your Inspired Life Fitness Trail

chapter five

Shall We Dance?

APPENDIX

welcome

I admire you.

Simply by picking up this book you are demonstrating an awareness and curiosity about taking your life to the next level of fulfillment and prosperity in tune with your true self. And, most likely, you have a willingness to actually go for it.

If you're feeling confused and don't really have a sense of the life you *do* want to create- relax and congratulations. Ironically, that can be a great place from which to start. The good news is that you are awake and open. If you do have a clear mission and want support in bringing that to life- congratulations again. You are also in the right place. This work will take you deeper, help you birth your vision, and create lasting success aligned with the real you.

My passion to equip people to wake up inspired is fueled by experience with hundreds of clients since 1996, decades of study with leading experts, and gratitude for how blessed I feel about my own life today. More and more people are asking, "How do I combine spiritual growth and real world achievement?" They want pragmatic *how-to* support, not just parables. Unfortunately, this is not really taught in school, on the job or hardly anywhere else. This book offers a roadmap and tools to begin that journey. What you hold in your hands was born out of a more comprehensive Wake Up Inspired program that's been road-tested in workshops and private coaching sessions through the years. With my clients, it's fascinating to keep learning more about what actually works in real lives over time. My hope is that this book will serve as a launch pad for reinventing your life, or be just enough for the rejuvenation boost you desire for now.

Dear reader, I wish to acknowledge your courage, self-compassion and motivation in choosing to embark on this path. I promise you that if you read this book, explore the tools, and make new choices integrating these principles into your life, you'll discover the gift of admiring yourself. People will wonder what that sparkle behind your eyes is all about. You'll smile and feel grateful for the adventure your life has become.

Let's begin.

A longing
for the
dance stirs
in the buried life.

Stanley Kunitz

chapter one
Waking Up to a New Story

And the day came when the risk
to remain tight in the bud
was more painful than
the risk it took to
blossom

Anais Nin

Why Wake Up Inspired?
A Revolution Brewing

I want to ask you something and tell you something.

The question is: *What are you living for?* If an observer watching your daily behavior were asked this question, what would he or she surmise?

And here's what I want to tell you: You were not born to settle. The purpose of your life was never supposed to be about getting all the to-do lists done or clinging to security. Your life was never meant to become a waiting room, either. You know, waiting for a prince or a pension to come? You're not supposed to feel stuck or restless. It is your destiny to enjoy a healthy body and spirit, to realize who you truly are and share your gifts in the world. The joyful life within your heart's desire is longing for you, wishing you'd listen more to its call.

There's no denying an epidemic of American female achievers feeling disenchanted or called toward a higher purpose (or both). I believe this healthy restlessness is part of a revolution brewing among awakening women. I don't mean any kind of hostile revolt, but a need to revolutionize how we pursue ambition and achievement. It's about enthusiastically taking a stand for healthier, smarter, more joyful success, for ourselves and for a sisterhood of conscious women.

Has it hit *you* yet? Do you love your life, or are you beginning to join the chorus of "*Is this all there is?*" on Monday mornings? You may hear that small, persistent voice from within that yearns for something deeper. It reminds you that you're meant to enjoy this ride and maybe even make a difference along the way. Rest assured, you are not alone in seeking authentic meaning and aliveness. Today, there is a distinct groundswell of people craving *soul satisfaction* in life and livelihood. Many reach a reflection and redirection juncture in their thirties and forties. Boomers hitting their fifties and sixties are seeking new ways to create that next phase of engaging in life rather than defaulting into outdated customs of retirement. Twenty-somethings are proactively interested in designing a balanced life that works and not waiting until midlife to ask the weighty "Why am I here?" questions. I believe that our so-called midlife crisis is evolving into a more optimistic series of life renewal passages.

I don't know if there is any age rule. You just feel ready and ripe for something more...something else. Women seem to arrive at this phase of thoughtful redesign earlier than men. Who knows exactly why. Perhaps it's all that time waiting in lines for ladies' rooms—forcing us to stop and take a good look at our life satisfaction.

For me, I reached a certain plateau while climbing the ladder of achievement and acquisition. My life appeared to be a smash success, at least from the outside looking in. I then began asking, "Now what?" Or more poignantly, "SO what?" Do you feel that strain in your life? Perhaps you feel unsure, torn between the desire to explore higher dreams and the urge to stay with sensible and secure routes. I knew I had to grab the next rung with more enthusiasm or dare a leap of faith into the unknown. But man, did I hang on in that bewildered discomfort for a long time.

I ended up grabbing a 3-month sabbatical that gave way to a deep performance review of how I was leading my life. I entered the stage of asking "*Is this what I really want? What am I meant to do with this lifetime? Is how I'm navigating smart and leading to joy, or am I heading toward a crash and burn?*" a bit ahead of schedule, in my early thirties.

To fast forward the story, I pried my white-knuckled fingers off that six-figure career ladder and reinvented my life. I've gone through phases of intense spiritual growth, immersion in holistic health, and slowing down. I've also resumed some speed, channeling my achievement energy into a thriving coaching practice as well as writing, teaching and speaking. This second act has a very different vibe. It's more like a calling than a career. It's what I've come to call a Joyful Mission. I am earning less money but enjoying a much richer life. It's hard to believe it's been almost ten years.

Especially because I love my life today, it breaks my heart to see so many of my "sisters" still feeling stuck, longing for more vitality and sense of purpose. I understand these women often feel they don't have enough time to get a haircut, never mind living up to their true destiny! I want to whisper, "Hey, it doesn't have to be that way."

Why Wake Up Inspired...Now?

This momentum toward craving higher fulfillment is particularly true among a group I call SAMMIES- Seeking Aliveness and Meaning, Mostly In Executive Suits. For years, I've noticed more and more achievers that are becoming seekers, predominantly among women. They are morphing into a hybrid of Seeker-Achievers.

Typically, they come from a white-collar, profit-priority, go-getting milieu. Now, they are increasingly intrigued with holistic health, inner wisdom, and contributing to something bigger than their CEO's (or their own) next bonus. A new fascination with spirituality has moved beyond the earthy, sandal-clad stereotype to more professionally oriented women with stylish heels and ambitious agendas.

I'm not the only one noticing these seismic shifts in our culture. Major media cover stories have spotlighted women who opt out of high profile, high pay careers for full time motherhood. Yet it soon became clear that "Family" isn't the only F word that deserves attention. Women crave more *fulfillment,* whether they have children or not. *Fast Company* magazine has reported that women aren't dropping out of business so much as creating their own version, starting new businesses at three times the rate of men. *Wall Street Journal* writer Sue Shellenbarger was so deluged with emails after writing one column on these issues that she was compelled to write the book *The Breaking Point: How Female Midlife Crisis is Transforming Today's Women.* The midlife crisis cliché has been about 40-ish men, red sports cars, trophy mistresses and hair plugs. New studies reveal that more women than men now experience a challenging midlife transition. This transition can either lead to despair or to the most amazing, rewarding time ever.

One conclusive theme emerges in reviewing recent studies and women's stories. It's not that women aren't powerful or talented enough to make it in the top rungs. Rather, many are *choosing* not to pursue lifestyles they view as hazardous to one's psychological, physical, spiritual and ethical health. Who wants to keep pushing to break through a glass ceiling if this leads to more stress and a shattered spirit? We are at the threshold of redefining success and reclaiming joy. I think professional women will and must lead this movement. This is great news for alert women willing to embrace change.

What about men? you might ask. I love men. I admire and adore working with my male clients. When there's a preponderance of women gathered, I'm inclined to declare that we need some testosterone to balance things out for more well-rounded perspectives. As a 40-something female with a white collar background, I am inherently more prepared to relate to similar women. Also, conscious professional women seem to be the most likely catalysts for a movement that says, "Hey, wait a minute. Are we really connected to our true selves, promoting the higher good?" (Of course their starter questions sound more like, "Yikes, can I keep juggling and struggling like this?!") It's our *feminine energy* (in both men and women) that urges us to slow down and tune in to more substance.

Why Wake Up Inspired…As Women?

There's a resurgence of feminine energy percolating with this desire to take a stand for healthier, more meaningful success. In the early nineties a number of best-selling books argued that the growing influence of women, especially in business, could help create a more humane and nurturing American culture. Since then, we certainly have more evidence to suggest that women should naturally feel, think and lead differently. You've probably seen the medical research revealing that the female brain is literally wired differently, and that we use both sides of our brains more holistically than men. Unfortunately, many clients and colleagues echo the refrain that pressure to be like a man in order to succeed "has gotten worse" in ten years, not better.

Whatever your admiration or resistance to the term *feminism,* let's agree to the benefits of reviving the power and pride of feminine energy. It's clear that the values and cultural undertow of professional life have many of us swimming against the current of our true nature. It's exhausting. Many women don't even know why they're feeling "out of sync," or realize that there are millions of other women out there feeling the very same way. How can we make it easier to *just love being a girl?*

This revolution that I speak of is a movement towards becoming whole and experiencing a harmony between who you are deep inside, and how you function in the outer world. "Life, liberty and pursuit of happiness" has a renewed echo in our hearts as we begin the 21th century. In the 19th and 20th century, the first feminist initiatives were about "Life" — I exist. I have a say in the world. I count and get a vote. "Liberty" overlaps nicely with the push for the freedom to pursue financial independence and equal opportunity to compete for the corner office. We have come a long way, baby, and owe much gratitude to our fore-sisters.

Nonetheless, it's not turning out how we dreamed once upon a time, is it? Now, we have a grand opportunity to revamp "The

Pursuit of Happiness." Let's pray we are wiser about what "happiness" entails and realize that she who dies with the most toys is probably spending too much time on eBay.

I'm also hopeful that more women will be inspired to nourish and support each other (rather than augment the unfortunate, power-hungry stereotypes that glorify survival of the self-promoting fittest). Part of the new wave of feminism should include breaking a code of pretense, being more honest with each other about how we actually feel, and supporting each other with genuine empathy.

We are still letting masculine dominance run the world. How well is that working? There is a profound need to awaken the nourishing qualities in all of us. There's more buzz around the divine feminine in spiritual circles. The planet needs our compassion and our fierce strength, like that mother bear energy, protecting her cubs. We need more feminine power actively engaged in the world to end violence and to feed the hungry. Feminine energy inspires us to include, revive and collaborate more than renounce, dominate and slaughter. Modern spiritual rebel-rouser, Marianne Williamson, has said that it is the *adult female* of a group who leads the way towards conscious change that can heal and protect the long-term survival of that species. Of course, we still want to celebrate all of the magnificent qualities of men, while bringing more women to the table. We need to encourage more feminine potency expressing itself in both genders, for the higher good of all people.

If we join our amazing hearts, brains and hands more, we can stir up a revolution. Imagine channeling our ambition into creative ways of inspiring ourselves and others. We can make a difference by infusing the best of feminine spirit into our lives, businesses and world leadership.

If all of this feels daunting, please exhale and relax. I can appreciate how you might be thinking, "I don't want to join a revolution or change the world...I just want to get a grip on creating a more rewarding life." Rest assured that this book is not a manifesto for a new feminist movement, an overhaul of the business world, or irate activism to save the planet. My calling is focused on equipping individuals like you to create more fulfilling, prosperous lives and careers. You can also trust that all of this change begins with making more breathing room and calm in your life, not with pushing and working harder. I do hope that — one person or small group at a time— this work will contribute to a larger movement, helping people to wake up to who they truly are and choose to contribute positive energy in newly conscious ways. Why not go for a trickle down theory of inspiration? Are you in?

When
sleeping
women
wake,
mountains move.

Chinese Proverb

Why Wake Up Inspired... as Human Beings?

What does it mean to wake up inspired, to live an inspired life? How do we fuel our inspired missions, creating inspired work, inspired relationships, inspired leadership, inspired businesses, inspired communities and inspired legacies? I have been blessed to realize that having an inspired life—allowing my true spirit to motivate every choice – is like the difference between struggling and climbing for things in life and letting the "lift" of your higher energy power your trip.

In the dictionary under "inspired" we find *aroused, animated...imbued with the spirit to do a certain thing, by or as by divine influence.* An archaic use of inspire is *to infuse breath and life.* It's interesting to see how this is distinct from "aspire" which means *to be eagerly desirous, especially for something of great value.* Inspired Living is infused with a different motivation, e.g. to contribute, rather than primarily to gain or stockpile. It informs how we show up in the world, how we treat ourselves and our neighbors down the block and across the human race.

Ironically, with all of our accumulation of technology and worldly advancement, we are experiencing a poverty of inspiration. We are not feeding our spirits enough. Lack of inspiration is expensive. Consider the ultimate cost of millions of uninspired workers who have lost that lovin' feeling. Notice the deficit of inspired or inspiring leaders, resulting in missed opportunities for a more robust economy and nourished environment. Lack of inspiration is a threat to our well-being, from personal health to the health of our global relationships. When we are not feeling inspired, we are operating from inertia, fear or feeling overwhelmed. What the world needs now is... inspiration.

Trends all around us are amplifying our inner desire for more wholeness and truth. Personal growth and spirituality books are best sellers across the country. Medical schools are espousing eastern philosophies that say thoughts, emotions and spirituality are vital components of health care and well being. This stuff isn't just for New Agers anymore, folks. Wake up and smell the herb tea. We are also witnessing a dismantling of institutions and assumptions that shakes our core. Shall we rewind and review? Consider September 11, corporate corruption, political scandals, biased media, pedophilia and cover ups in the Catholic Church, and trials that test our faith in the American justice system. Add to that Iraq, mind-blowing natural disasters, watching our retirement savings wither, and seeing our friends go unemployed.

As miserable as it all sounds, we can still find the gift here. Something is telling us to be more aware, less complacent. Underneath the headlines, there's an invitation to remember who we are as souls and to revere, care for and lift up each other. The human spirit is feisty. Notice how wake up calls prompt you and the people around you to re-evaluate priorities and seek more deeply chosen lives. We have a dramatic opportunity to collectively create a more accepting, fulfilling, harmonious world. You and I say we want peace (and other good things for ourselves and the planet), but may feel baffled as to how to actually influence something that vast. I now believe in the song lyrics, "Let there be peace on earth *and let it begin with me*" with every cell of my being. If each of us embarks on this inspired path earnestly, it changes everything—how you see yourself and everyone else you encounter, what matters and what is unnecessary drama. I am humbled at the peace I feel in my own life and fascinated with amazing possibilities for our brighter future.

It's Time for a New Story

What kind of world could we develop if more of us really did wake up inspired and fell asleep grateful? It is time for a provocative conversation that goes beyond "success" and beyond "balance." Transcending both of these, we can find the rewarding mission each of us is destined to lead. It is time for a series of shifts, from autopilot achievement and consumption to conscious choices, from overload to wholeness, from vague restlessness to enthusiastically living on purpose.

It is time to wake up and claim who you are meant to become.

So, how does one get started? First, stop rushing. Time flies whether we're having fun or not. Hit the pause button. Stop long enough to take a good look at your life. Notice the choices that have landed you in your current situation and your current state of being— mind, body and spirit.

Once upon a time, I refused to slow down. (I could have been a poster girl for *Women Who Work Too Much and the Companies that Love Them*.) My body got my attention with some health challenges that encouraged me to examine my choices. Soon after taking the leap of quitting my job (yet busy again with a new consulting gig), my brother-in-law, uncle and mother were all rushed to the hospital within a span of a few days. I recall shuffling through my fifth airport in 48 hours like a zombie, not able to stifle tears, trying to reach my mother in time to say goodbye. My mother died and of course, the loss was devastating. Yet, somewhere in the fog of grief, there was that beacon, reminding me that I could no longer afford to wait to follow my heart and start living *my life*.

My husband Kelly and I took a trip to Florida shortly after my mother's death. I quietly strolled the beach and noticed how many "old people" seemed to be too ill or frail to really enjoy these so-called golden years. It prompted me to think that our cultural agreement of working our brains out for decades with a tilt-o-whirl lifestyle and then retiring to some sunny playground in our late 60's was just *backasswards*.

I wondered too if my mother had really experienced enough joy in her life. I wanted to have her back, to argue over losing each other at the shopping mall, to giggle over her accidentally saying "discharge" instead of "discard" while playing cards, and maybe to ask her what she would have done differently with her life. I couldn't bring my mother back, but I could certainly resurrect passion, purpose and joy in my own life, and maybe even in other people's lives somehow. I was only 34 and I didn't want to plan for enjoying life more thirty years later.

Please don't wait for a crisis to be your wake up call. Life is short and precious. You have the power within you now to create the life you deserve. Where you go from here is another grand choice. Just asking yourself "Is this how I really want to live?" (rather than sleep-walking through the status quo) is a significant step toward shaping an inspired life for yourself. Remember you are not alone. Also keep in mind that you never know what your life might look like a few years or even months from now. *Your* joy is waiting around the corner.

Is the life I'm living *the life that wants*
to live in me?

Parker Palmer

Why Don't We Live More Inspired Lives?

Why on earth do we linger in lifestyles and careers that don't fortify and delight us? Often we need a catalyst for change, like the death of a loved one or being reorganized out of a career path. Without intense wake up calls, we can be like frogs slowly boiled to death, not realizing the water temperature is gradually increasing. We go along with the schedule, pay the mortgage and answer emails while calendar pages fly and our souls wither a tiny bit each day. We also tell ourselves convincing stories about not having enough time, money or courage.

There are legitimate obstacles from outside sources. Nonetheless, we trip ourselves up with our own beliefs that block inspiration and prosperity. In my Wake Up Inspired workshops I often ask, "What's getting in the way of living a life you would love?" The underlying reasons include old wounds, patterns from one's family of origin, fears about security, leaving known routines for the riskier unknown, lack of encouragement, vagueness and inertia.

There are worthwhile tools for dealing with resistance and taming our self-sabotage. However, the most expedient way is often to leapfrog over these obstacles with passion and faith. All of the structures for focus, prioritization and action follow-through will grind and squeak without the lubrication of your passion and faith. Passion and faith combine in a recipe for inspiration. You can choose to create a new story.

The following chart is another look at the shift toward the new story of Inspired Success. The left side of the chart represents some ways we have tried to create success. Let's call this the "old story" that clearly doesn't lead to joy. The right side represents an inspired path that many people are finding to be a more authentic choice. Each side may be exaggerated a bit to show contrast, yet this doesn't stray too far from reality. Scan and see for yourself what new choices are calling to you.

"Old Story" Success Track	Inspired Success, A New Story
"Accommodating Overachiever" Nose-to-grindstone workhorse, striving to get ahead.	"Seeker-Achiever" Intentional, values and purpose-driven, on a Joyful Mission.
Busy, busy, busy. Often running on autopilot, feeling overwhelmed.	May be busy, yet well-paced. Conscious, tuning-in to assess her course often enough.
Sacrificing personal well-being for work, family, doing for others.	Personal health, well-being are highly valued and life habits walk the talk.
Aspires to make more money.	Inspired to make a difference.
"Never enough" inner driver pushes her to be overly responsible. People pleasing and perfectionism may kick in.	Aligned, appropriate responsibility. More inner-directed. A balanced sense of "enough" while still honoring values of excellence.
Driven by proving herself and getting ahead.	Guided by her higher power to joyfully serve.
Slave to her to-do list, starting to feel trapped.	Master of conscious choices, feeling on path.
Squeezes in salon visits as a treat when she's exhausted. Thinks about going to personal growth workshop, doesn't sign up or follow through.	Practices proactive wellness and positive success-fueling habits. Has a personal & professional coach, massage therapist, regular exercise regime, et al.
Knows Chardonnays and the Wall Street Journal.	Also knows Chakras and Yoga Journal.
Post it note on computer says, "Just Do It" (with Do it ALL implied).	Post it note reads, "BREATHE."
Tries to execute a logical strategic plan.	Incorporates intuition and metaphysical principles into how she navigates through life and work.
Climbing to the top of the ladder for financial wealth, power and acclaim.	Dancing with her destiny, fueling truly prosperous, rewarding work and life.
Exercises at the gym for the sake of stamina, peak performance.	Exercises for the sake of wellness and optimal energy flow. Overlaps with her spiritual growth.
Trying to juggle it all.	Assessing choices and building her dream team of support.
Loves shoes.	Loves shoes. ☺

OK, so now you see (at the end of the chart) that I'm asserting that we can be on a quest for higher consciousness and a great shoe sale in the same lifetime. Also, I'm not telling you to quit your job and go meditate on a mountain in order to wake up inspired. The key is to bring inspiration *to* your life and work, often with healthier habits and a deeper connection to your inner guidance. Apply the concepts throughout the rest of the book to your career, relationships and other aspects of life. That's how you'll get to enjoy having both a healthy, joyful spirit and your ambitious achievement as well.

Take a moment to ask yourself what resonates with you from the chart. What might be the key ingredients of your "old story" and "new story" shifts?

Where There's *Inspiration,* There's a Way

Essentially, the new story is Inspired Living. An inspired person taps into a way of living intentionally, consciously and creatively. Let me attempt to further define these words in the context of Inspired Living:

Intentional = On purpose. Inherently fueled by awareness of values and true priorities. By design, not default.

Conscious = Awake. Tuned-in to guidance. Surrender and co-creation with Spirit. Passion-fueled. Compelled by callings more than driven by ego-based goals. Spirited.

Creative = Actually creating, building, manifesting in the real world. Mission and vision in action. Playing with possibilities (e.g. "How could I/we...?" rather than "When will they...?" or "I/ we can't...")

An inspired person is authentically ambitious, up to something, contributing positive energy to humankind in his or her own unique way. Don't jump only to save-the-world, living-on-granola (or wealthy philanthropist) stereotypes. There are a gazillion ways to have a valuable impact in virtually any field, lifestyle, community, or income level.

Another important mark of Inspired Living is that it is always looking for the good. It is imbued with curiosity and good humor, finding the lesson or growth in everything. It chooses to be happy and rejoices each day, now. It is highly receptive. Being a clear channel to let Spirit (or God or Love or other names) express is a top priority. It trusts that we are well held within something greater, and responsible for contributing to something greater. It lives brightly in "What if?" positive possibilities.

To choose an inspired life, you need to carve out a clearing in all the limiting beliefs, excuses and habit patterns you have collected as your "old story." (Not eliminate them, just cut a slit opening at first, if that's where you are.) Then, you get real with yourself and ask the Magic Question:

"Am I willing to love myself enough to create the life I am meant to lead? "

If it were as simple as saying yes to this, we'd all be living out our joyful missions already. So, the fundamental Magic Formula is:

- **Self-Love**

- **Structure**

- **Support**

If self-love is a bit too warm and fuzzy for you, replace it with self-care, self-respect, or whatever language suits you. Self discipline is useful, but not all by itself and not if it's mostly punitive. The longer I do this work, the more I imagine our various Angel teams having a coffee break somewhere, sighing, "I wish they would just love themselves more." We are the ones struggling to be good, achieve more and try harder with linear logic. What we really need is to lighten up, be more compassionate (toward ourselves and others), and know that a loving higher power wants us to succeed. A prerequisite for Inspired Living is to choose to be a self-loving, self-respecting person. That's not an elective.

Structure comes in the form of cultivating lifestyle rituals and specific commitments for developing insights and new behaviors. This might be as simple as scheduling appointments with yourself in your calendar to devote time to your personal development work. You will choose what works best for your unique conditions and aspirations.

Support is a critical ingredient. We all know this intellectually. It's fascinating how often we don't fully practice it. It makes an immense difference to have non-judgmental sounding boards, brainstorm partners, and champions who believe in you *and* hold you accountable. This could be a professional coach, support buddy or group. Avoid "support groups" that devolve into a cry-into-your-beer fest or over-coddling the weakest, teariest member. I'm talking about an empowerment group that is both nurturing and challenging. Most of all, you want a coach, buddy or group that inspires you to boost positive growth toward becoming who you are meant to be. The exercises throughout the book are set up for you to be able to dive in and gain momentum on your own. If you'd like ideas about how to find a coach, or form a group, there's more information in the appendix.

• • • Hit the Pause Button: Take a Breath • • •

At the beginning of each coaching session, my clients and I take a breath. It may sound insignificant yet simply taking in a good deep breath has multiple benefits. Right now, breathe in through your nose, hold it for a moment, and breathe out through your mouth. Repeat this a few times until you notice feeling a little more calm, grounded and present. I like to breathe at the start of coaching simply to segue from whatever the client has been doing - to choose to "be here" for the session and really gain value. It's amazing how something as simple as breathing can actually shift your state of being throughout the day—to help you focus, gain perspective, make a thoughtful decision, prevent yourself from saying something you might regret and so on.

One of the most powerful ways to Hit the Pause Button is to ask yourself, *What would I like to exhale out? What would I like to breathe in?*

This quick tool can be quite profound. It's an efficient "state of the union" check for how you are feeling and managing your energy. During coaching, it often bypasses the "stories" and gets to the core of what needs attention. Client examples include:

Exhale out "confusion." Breathe in "clarity and focus."
Exhale out "overwhelmed." Breathe in "trusting my intuition."
Exhale out "distraction, coasting." Breathe in "100% engaged in what I'm up to."

Reflect on whatever you'd like to release (or have less of), and what you'd like to invite into your life in terms of your thoughts, feelings and energy. You'll notice how this zeroes in on what is really "up" for you. It's a great little laser tool you can easily implement.

Pause right now and actually exhale out and breathe in with *your* desires in mind. There's something real about releasing the stagnant energy with your exhale and mindfully inhaling your intentions. What perspective shift or tangible action would allow more of what you want? As an example, my client Donna wanted to exhale out "feeling trapped" and breathe in "taking care of me." We discussed how some of her commitments might be aligned with her values. This helped shift her perspective. She recognized how she could choose things aligned with her priorities rather than feel trapped by a sense of obligation. Also, we agreed to tangible actions, such as creating stronger boundaries to protect her exercise time. Both of these helped her feel more at peace about taking care of herself.

I also urge you to trust that small, incremental insights and behavior modifications do indeed create a cumulative shift. My client Eileen reported with pleasant surprise at how working the "Hit the Pause Button" tool created positive shifts in her experience of life after only a couple weeks. She had been thoughtfully taking five minutes each morning. She experimented with consciously choosing what to *exhale out and breathe in* in the middle of work meetings. She realized that the effort didn't need to be huge to make a difference.

Small acts
really can
add up to big
transformation.

Lynn Redenour

From Inspiration to Real Life Application

We have established that there's a movement brewing about creating more inspired lives. This applies to you personally as well as to the future of women, our socio-economic health, and the well-being of the planet. Mostly, I hope you are inspired to commit to becoming more intentional, and to loving yourself enough to go for it. Understandably, where most people get stuck is "How?" Many self-help platitudes about happiness are enjoyable, but they are not useful enough for the smart seeker-achiever who genuinely wants to fuel positive change.

In the next chapter, we begin to lay the ground work for how to create inspired lives, both philosophically and pragmatically. I wish I had that magic pill to instantly transform your life, or the three easy steps to have it all done within 10 days. There is no such pill. You've already seen those quick-easy-steps self-help books and know they don't really do the whole job.

This book includes plenty of practical application tools and exercises. To give you a real chance at creating the inspired life you deserve, we must first equip you with key conceptual foundations. Be willing to stretch your beliefs. Be willing to postpone immediate gratification at times. Hang in there for the higher payoff of creating sustainable, inspired success.

Smart Set Up for Using This Book

From this point on, you'll have many chances to apply concepts to your own life. Of course, I want you to have a great return on the time and energy you invest in your first dip into the Wake Up Inspired work. And, just as I would encourage you to create your inspired life in your own way, please take in these concepts and tools at your own pace and in your own style. You could scan the entire book and then select what resonates most to adapt into your day-to-day living. Even if you picked up only one new idea, such as a morning ritual or a new walking habit, this will have an impact. If you'd like to gain more value, commit to working with this material over about 90 days, engaging in a new exercise each week. There's a 13-week suggested schedule in the Appendix for your consideration.

Let's touch on preventing feeling overwhelmed, and on smart set up. When clients start coaching or begin the Wake Up Inspired (WUI) course, it's important to recognize how much room they have to take in a whole new set of ideas and homework assignments. So, take a moment to reflect on your capacity. Remember Lucy and Ethel in that famous episode of *I Love Lucy*, frantically working at the conveyer belt of chocolates? Can you imagine telling Lucy to mediate and delegate more at that moment, without changing the speed of those chocolates coming in? At the same time, we wouldn't want Lucy to be doomed to a life of continued panic, either. You need to hit the pause button at some point.

As we move forward, bear in mind what will help you gain the most value. What are the most compassionate and smart ways to set yourself up to succeed? (This is a great question to apply to several areas of your life, by the way.) You already know the difference between just reading a book like this and truly attempting to integrate the tools. So, get a notebook with plenty of lined paper and dedicate it to your Wake Up Inspired exercises. Consider duplicating the following chart to capture your key learnings, intentions, support and follow through. This is a "Structure and Support" tool.

Topic Area	My Key Insights	Possible applications—How I'd like to integrate this into my life	What's Next? Commitments, Intentions	Accountability Support & Check In Comments

"What's Next?" could include tangible actions or questions to ponder. Be specific and use your calendar. As an example, note the difference between a commitment to "enhance my self care" versus a scheduled commitment to walk out in the fresh air for 20 minutes at lunchtime on Monday, Wednesday and Friday (Structure).

To take it a step further, make an agreement with a trusted person or group to be held accountable. Research shows that specific, scheduled accountability check-ins with another person increase your chances of actually doing something by as much as 85 percentage points. Add your friend Jane as an accountability buddy and commit to sending her an email by end of day Friday, reporting in about walking (Support). You can also use "Check-In Comments" to acknowledge progress and recognize what you are learning about yourself, your patterns of behavior, what works well in your life and so on. Be sure to celebrate your progress in new awareness. Gaining insight into what makes you tick and how to best fuel your continued growth is often more important than just tracking explicit action steps.

OK, let's start off with a party for your first exercise. Grab your notebook and a cup of tea, if you like. The dress code for this party is come as you are. Or maybe come as you are becoming.

• • • • • • Happy Birthday! • • • • • •

Let's take a little trip in time. Close your eyes and imagine being the invisible woman at your 90th birthday party. You're healthy and look great. Take in all the sights, smells, tastes, sounds and other sensations. You can easily eavesdrop and observe. You can magically sense what the 90-year-old birthday girl is feeling and thinking. Scan each question below, and then close your eyes to *return to the party*. When you sense your answers coming, open your eyes and write your insights in your WUI notebook. (Repeat this for each question.)

Recalling your life, you are most *pleased and proud* of how you have invested your energy how/where?

It's making your heart sing to hear people say _____ _____about you and how knowing you has touched them. (Work, Family, Friends, Community, other?)

What might you regret?

At this age, looking back on your life, you realize that what matters most is _____.

Now, imagine the wise 90-year-old you compassionately giving you advice, relevant to where you are in time right now. Know that she loves you and wants the best for you. Imagine hearing her guidance (and fill in the blank).

She says, (Your Name), for your life's growth, it is time for you to _____.

Often people attempt
to live their lives backwards;
        They try to have more things, more money,
in order to do more of what they want
                so that they will be happier.

        The way it actually works
is the reverse.
        You must first be
                who you really are,
                then do what you need to do,
        in order to have what you want.

Margaret Young

chapter two
Having a Plan is Not the Answer

How Do We Create Inspired Lives?

When I ask new clients what they'd love to get out of coaching, a popular answer is "I want a plan." They want "control" and to work on "setting goals" and then execute the "to-do steps" with new and improved will power. We'd all like *the plan* that will make everything brighter and easier. I confess that it's tempting for me to jump in to create a strategic plan with them. After all, my clients are bright, successful grownups and their initial desires are not naive. However, coaching human beings each week of their lives has dramatically convinced me that *having a plan is not the answer.*

I absolutely believe in being more deliberate with creating your life, but that's not the same thing as following a plan. I want you to set yourself up to flourish. Frankly, no one experiences transformation to a joyful life primarily from a strategic plan. A variation on this plan-and-control theme is "All I need is superior will power." Expecting yourself to change or do something by sheer determination is a cruel entrapment. Cooperating with your inner guidance and co-creating with the right *energy* are more worthwhile pursuits.

My life has not played out according to the scripts I wrote. Has yours? We have all experienced this truth: even when you plan well, you can always count on change and unexpected distractions – as well as wonderful opportunities never figured into your plans. Don't worry, we are not throwing away the idea of a plan. We're improving on it.

Like many of you, I've been around the personal and professional growth block for decades. Now that I have coached and led workshops with hundreds of clients over the years, I have a humbling, profound appreciation for what actually works in real lives in the modern world.

In this chapter, I share the key foundations for Inspired Living.

In these foundations we delve into reconnecting to who you are and understanding what does and does not create joy. To truly flourish in the 21st century, we need to learn how to blend the best of spirituality and "right brain" principles with "left brain" pragmatism. We also need to cultivate an ongoing cycle of making *optimal choices*, amidst whatever life throws our way. Better still is to have these choices inspired by our core values and infused by a deeper mind-body-spirit integration. We're going to cover each of these key foundations in a bit more depth and then bring it all together in one, integrated structure I call the Inspired Life Fitness Trail.

A primary reason that seeking control, setting goals and planning don't lead to inspired lives is the order in which we pursue them. "How are we going to get there?" should be the final question, not the first. If we ask "Where do you want to go?" or "What do you really want?" we still haven't mined the real treasure. A potential snag in this level of goal setting concerns *who you are* when you attempt to answer these questions.

My husband recalls a Gilligan's Island episode in which Gilligan is in position to gain a huge sum of money. The skipper asks him what he'd love to do with this windfall. "A skateboard and ten pounds of licorice!" Gilligan replies.

"Hey, little buddy, you need to think bigger," Skipper says.

Gilligan tries again. "OK, a fleet of skateboards and twenty pounds of licorice!"

Of course you're way more sophisticated. Still, we all have some degree of Gilligan consciousness. We have self-imposed limits about what's possible, influenced by decades of conditioning.

It's also fascinating to watch how "getting what you want" does not usually bring genuine fulfillment. Achieving what our egos want (or being *driven* by various external influences) is often counter-productive when you are seeking a wonderfully soul-satisfying life. Imagine the big promotion at work or the lake house ultimately turning into more pressure than pleasure.

How do we access the deeper, truer answers? For that, we need to begin with a more penetrating question. A better starting point is "Who do I want to be?" The enriched version of this is "Who am I meant to be?" This isn't exactly the question that crosses our minds in the day-to-day rushing around, nor is it encouraged by our workplaces, family, friends or TV sets.

And this question is the key to your inspired life.

Reconnecting to Who You Are

The truth of who you are is already within you. I wish this didn't sound like a cute Zen bumper sticker. It is the most important, paradoxically simple and complex message I can pass on. A subtle inner knowing contains all of the answers that can lead you to your highest possibilities.

You can feel well-held by a loving universe and guided to move forward with a "yes" or a "no" to every choice, both tiny and huge. Whether you think of this as looking within yourself or as seeking God's will is up to you, of course. These don't need to be competing concepts. You don't need to feel separate from your higher power. This inner guidance is your connection to the greater All, however this feels true and works for you.

If you are reading this book, you are a seeker in some way. While seeking implies looking all around, trying to figure things out, the most efficient route is to inquire within. Literal trips to far off lands can serve as wonderful catalysts for your inner journey work, but it's not the mountain or the retreat center that holds your answers. You won't find *the* formula in the "Change Your Life in 10 Minutes a Day" audio program either.

The keys to your highest good and most beneficial ways of operating are inside of you. If we could just tap into all this directly, we would never need life purpose courses or nutritional plans laid out by someone else. Your body wisdom knows what to eat, how to move and when to rest for your best possible energy flow and vibrant health. Your heart intelligence knows the gifts you are meant to share, your true work, and the relationships you are meant to engage in during this lifetime. This notion of being in sync with your true spirit is the epitome of *simple but not easy*. So, we do need tools - real, thought-provoking tools with lasting effects - to help us peel away the layers of programming and habits that distract us from our own truth.

This inner knowing is what gives you a fire in your belly and wakes you up at 4 A.M. with a thought you must write down, or a dream with an important message for you. Maybe you have not experienced your true spirit in quite these ways, but you know it when you feel it. At one end of the spectrum you have peak moments of completely losing track of time, of being so connected to who you are and everything that's meant to be, that you feel more alive than you can describe. Far from this are those times when we feel trapped, beyond bored, or stuck in a life pattern that gives new meaning to "near death experience."

Imagine that your inner truth could direct and propel you, while your choices just naturally flowed in sync with this highest expression all of the time. You would not experience doubt or confusion. Imagine a world in which everyone was so tuned in to their own true spirit that we all felt at peace and "on path." We would gratefully and eagerly show up each day to keep fueling each other and celebrate the evolution of the planet. People would not feel attracted to the worst of human nature as news or entertainment. There would be no need for any societal structures or industries stemming from lack, fear or screw your neighbor. We would remember our connectedness across borders and beliefs. To access your own center of truth and to open up that world of possibility, you need to expand beyond your five senses and logical, culturally-pressured formulas. You want to start dancing with your destiny more.

Let's get pragmatic about how to cultivate that connection to your inner truth on a more consistent basis. One of the fundamental Wake Up Inspired tools is Tune In Time. My first invitation is to not overcomplicate or over-mystify this. I have avoided labeling this "Meditation Time" quite intentionally. The word "meditation" often brings up expectations and unspoken rules about how it should be done or how one should feel during the experience. Please don't let that baggage rob you of a very simple, essential tool for letting your joyful life unfold. Create your own unique language for this, if that inspires you. Client examples include Rejuvenating Communion, Conversation with God, and Connecting with My Wise Self.

One of the best ways to Tune In is to close your eyes and breathe. Isn't it nice to know that this tool is always with you? No appointment, special training or equipment needed. Just sit comfortably and relax your shoulders. Keep your spine straight. Breathe in through your nose and out through your mouth. With your Tune In practice, you're hitting the pause button not just to unplug, but to *listen*. You are tuning in to your heart, your inner voice, true spirit guidance, and sensory experiences beyond the traditional five senses.

I used to think I had failed *Meditation 101*. In spite of hearing a workshop leader say that there was no such thing as bad meditating, I was convinced I must be doing it wrong. Sitting still just made my busy brain whirl even more and then I'd feel frustrated rather than relaxed. (Of course this is when I'd assume everyone else must be experiencing Nirvana after a few deep breaths and I was the only imbecile who just couldn't get it.) If this resonates with you, cut yourself some slack and know that most people feel this way when first trying a Tune In Time practice. Don't panic or beat yourself up for those busy thoughts. If we *try hard* to empty the mind, chances are the distracting thoughts will actually increase. If sitting with your eyes closed while focusing on your breath seems to cause more aggravation than alignment at first, try giving yourself something to "do." Stare at a candle flame or listen to a piece of soothing music.

This may feel silly or pointless at first. Be patient. Stick with it. Don't expect to experience lightening bolt clarity or mystic messages from the other side. Just start with focusing on your breathing. Keep it simple. Try this for five minutes each day for a week or so. If it feels right, build up to ten minutes or more over time. Do not start at forty-five minutes. This is one of those *Tortoise and the Hare* situations where the overachiever approach flashes early and fizzles out too soon, while the slow, steady, incremental increases over time build a sustainable practice.

Also, you don't have to sit still to Tune In. That's another rule we erroneously impose on ourselves. Let's demystify the whole "sitting and being still" thing. It's only one way of tuning in, not *the* way. Consider walking in a serene setting. Try stretching, bending and moving with your eyes closed, or anything else that will facilitate your capacity to *be* and tune inward.

To help you nurture your new habit, keep a daily Tune In Time diary in your notebook for a few weeks. You could simply make a checkmark for each Tune In Time, or add comments and an accountability agreement with someone, if you like.

Date	Tune In Time	Comments/ Accountability Support

It's natural to have some starts and stops along the way in trying to cultivate Tune In Time as a part of your daily routine. It takes practice, patience, and playing around with various structures to discover your own way of tuning in. Try using the diary log until your habit feels more natural, like brushing your teeth.

Every blade of grass
has its Angel that bends
over it and
whispers,
"Grow, grow."

The Talmud

Finding the Joy

Many wise teachers have told us that our purpose is to *enjoy* our lives. I'd like to make a distinction between enjoyment and joy. What could it mean to live primarily for enjoyment? Our culture seduces us into seeking pleasure and always chasing more—travel, gourmet cuisine, bigger and bigger homes, hot tubs, parties and self-pampering. Have you noticed the teen girl T-shirts at the mall that flash, "It's All About Me" and "Naughty, Spoiled Angel"? I get that it's tongue-in-cheek humor, yet I'm troubled by an underlying message that adds fire to looking for joy in all the wrong places. The pseudo-enlightened version of enjoyment might look like spa retreats, having a meditation garden built, expensive organic foods, exotic trips with famous gurus, and creating affirmations for all the pleasures you desire. Any variation of this fairy tale falls short of true fulfillment. You know deep inside of you that joy does not come from hedonistic pursuits of self-comfort, pleasure and financial gain. I invite you to seek true JOY rather than enjoyment. *So, how do we achieve joy?* Here is the vital key:

Authentic joy comes from sharing your true gifts.

This naturally involves knowing who you are meant to be and letting that true spirit express in the world. That's the real treasure, infinitely more fulfilling than our naive notions of pleasure or happiness. The way to enjoy the ride is to serve others and invest your energy in service of something that truly matters to you. If you only feed yourself, you will end up with an empty hunger. If you seek to nourish yourself for the sake of feeding others, you will experience sustenance beyond gratification. You will feel truly full.

I could say that I already know your life purpose and your gift. Your life purpose is joy. The deepest and highest gift you bring is love. I don't mean romantic love, but rather that *infinite power of love* expressing through you. Your unique expression of love is yours to discover and unleash. Since the universe is so darn loving, some pleasure seeking is a way to open up to knowing what your true gifts are. To be strong leaders, we often need to start with understanding and caring for ourselves more. Your first small step for humankind might be a pedicure and an afternoon off!

Let's make a clear distinction between self-absorption and the pursuit of self-realization. I once heard a radio interview with a Buddhist teacher who was making a point about the downside of all of this preoccupation around *What do I need? What do I want?* Since my life's work encourages people to ask these kinds of questions, I was intrigued. Who could argue with the pitfalls of too much self-absorption and not enough concern for love thy neighbor? Nonetheless, there is a paradox to be recognized here. I fervently believe that some level of fascination with yourself is necessary. It's a valid part of the journey towards being able to share the gifts that are meant to benefit others. We need to fill our own wells in order to give freely. What would we rather have— a world full of people attempting to love others because they feel they should, or a world full of people who can't help loving and contributing because it has become their natural joy to do so?

Finally, we don't *get* joy. It's not a destination at which we finally arrive. There's no red dot marking joy and its expedient routes on the map of life. It's an experience, a state of being, a consciousness and a path. To uncover your true gifts you'll want to align with what's *meant* to express through you. Imagine discovering an owner's manual for your soul- as if it's been in the glove compartment (and you never really read it thoroughly).

To experience the elation of contributing from your true spirit, you need to understand more of *who* you are. Thus the whole process is J.O.Y., or the Journey Of You.

Take some time to reflect on these questions and write some early insights in your notebook. Come from a place of gentle curiosity, without any pressure to figure it out.

How have you possibly tried to chase happiness and become disillusioned?

What resonates with you about "sharing your true gifts" as the key to finding joy? When have you felt a taste of authentic joy while being your best self and serving something greater than yourself?

How does the distinction of "self-absorption" and "self-realization" apply to you personally?

> Your own self-realization
> is the greatest service
> you can render the
> world.
>
> *Ramana Maharishi*

Finding Your Optimal Blend

As I was purging clutter one day, two old magazine covers caught my attention. *Working Woman* featured a very aggressive woman's face, mouth open, teeth bared like a lion's roar. "More Money Now!" and "Wall Street Success" yelled in large, hard-edged type. Beside this was *New Age* magazine (now titled *Body & Soul*) with a gentle, serene face and softer colors. The headline read, "Finding Your True Spiritual Path." The juxtaposition of these covers (that had fallen side by side) fascinated me. What about a middle path?

At first I guessed that the *Working Woman* issue was from the late eighties and the *New Age* cover more recent. In fact they were both from the spring of 1999. We have been struggling with these competing energies for long enough now, haven't we? The whole work/life balance conversation is one we've been having for decades, and it's getting tired and ineffective.

This conundrum too often gets framed as a binary conflict, as if we have only two options. Option A: Work like crazy in a dog-eat-dog world and sacrifice your soul. Option B: Drop out to hang out in Tai Chi class and find your true spiritual center. Trade in your *Wall Street Journal* for *Yoga Journal* and turn in your executive badge forever. Those "never look back" panty-hose burning fantasies are appealing in the early stages of life after corporate over-achievement. We leave our treadmill lifestyles to seek rest and contemplation for a while. However, bright, conscious women need some creative, challenge-thriving energy to stay alive. It's an essential part of the higher fulfillment we crave.

Option C could be the Mommy track, which has received plenty of attention as an admirable way of jumping off the rat wheel. Not all women are meant to have children. But we all are destined to give birth to something in the world. In my coaching work, it is my privilege and delight to play *mission midwife* for my clients, helping them to court callings, get pregnant with a deeper purpose, birth visions into life, continue to grow and fuel current missions in action.

Most of the women I encounter want stimulating, yet saner and more satisfying alternatives to the *work-'til-you-drop* or *completely unplugged* models. They want to achieve a balance between healthy challenge and chilling out. They want to combine achievement with meaning, ambition with spiritual grounding.

Ten years ago, it did feel like I had to choose to leave the land of reading spreadsheets to visit places that might read my aura. Today, I'm fascinated with what it is to create a blend of spirituality, health, and wisdom with real-world achievement. Rather than a tug-of-war, what is that optimal middle path fusion, combining the best of both worlds? How can spiritual consciousness and ambition in action be great dance partners?

Professional women are an intriguing breed. We engage in provocative conversations, challenging each other on topics ranging from innovation in business to breast feeding, soul fulfillment to spring fashion, hormones to homeland security. We care about the environment and evolution of our species, people development *and* profit margins. The emerging Seeker-Achiever might read stock reports and mystic poetry, attend executive board meetings and energy-balancing Reiki sessions. We are fascinated with learning about talent retention for leadership development and Tarot readings for psychic development. I am one example of this new hybrid species, if you will. I enjoy magazines like *Spirituality & Health* and *Fast Company*.

We don't aspire to build empires underscored by greed. Nor do we aspire to hang out in purple tights and beads, chanting for bliss all day, while struggling to pay the mortgage. It's more intriguingly complex than just, "Do we make money or feed our souls?" On the pure seeker's path, we might feel guilty about ambition, or lose our appetite for formerly ego-driven goals. As Seeker-Achievers, we can see the value in channeling some of our ambitious, business-like energy into tangible actions for higher good and meaningful impact. What we really want is wholeness, blending the best of both worlds (and both sides of our brain) for deep inspiration and constructive productivity.

The Seeker-Achiever in us is like Goldilocks, looking for the just right temperature for her porridge. We want to find the just right pace and ingredients for creating a life that works. My heart's desire is to let you know that you do have like-minded sisters out there. I love to help you find each other and equip you to *integrate* the best of holistic wellness, spiritual growth and professional ambition.

It is like integrative medicine, blending the best of western medical technologies with alternative healing modalities. We can use the right principles and tools for various purposes, from correcting cash flow to clearing chakras. It is a fascinating adventure to blend the following:

Five Sensory, Strategic Thinking	+	Six Sensory, Intuition, Prayer
Linear, Logical, Practical	+	Metaphysical, Mystical, Magical
Planning Ahead	+	Being in the Moment
Facts	+	Faith
Power, Gains	+	Purpose, Service
Increasing Speed	+	Slowing Down
Proactive Progress	+	Going With the Flow
External Style	+	Inner Substance
Winning, Go For It	+	Sacrifice, Surrender, Let Go
Play a Bigger Game	+	Simplify
Create, Build Up & Out	+	Quiet Down, Go Within

Consider the above two columns as "left" and "right" sides of how we operate. Let me share some examples of this blend in action.

Many clients begin coaching saying that they are at a crossroads, eager to find their second career path. If we focused on the "left side" operating style, we'd identify logical skills, and how to get him or her into the highest paying job as quickly as possible. Our process would be a linear progression of intellectual discussions, facts and figures. If we went to the extreme "right side," we might send this client to a silent meditation retreat for a month and then just surrender to whatever showed up in his or her life, without further discussions or proactive actions.

Where Passion Meets Profit

OK, it's obvious you want a middle ground. Together with my clients, we've developed a passion-meets-profit process that blends head and heart, logic and magic. You may have heard the phrase, "Do what you love, the money will follow." (This is also the title of a book by Marsha Sinetar). In my first month of coaching, I was concerned that people might be too idealistic about this catchy phrase. That compelled me to develop a more well-rounded model that started with four basic quadrants: a) passions, b) gifts, c) needs "in the world," and d) profit- what others are willing to pay for. After gaining insights about each of the quadrants, we can compose livelihood scenarios (passion + gift + a need met + profit = rewarding mission/career idea).

Our cultural conditioning steers most people to skip this process and go immediately to that fourth quadrant: What jobs exist out there? What have I typically been paid to do? You actually want to start by asking "What are my passions? What do I care about deeply? What could have me waking up inspired?"

Answering these questions is not exactly like answering, "What's your favorite color?" An approach that blends logic with a bit of mystery encourages clients to tap into their intuition or inner guidance. This may include slowing down and practicing patience to let insights occur, rather than racing to figure it all out. Even things like physical movement or eating habits can affect your ability to access true callings (in non-linear ways). Less sugar in your diet might help you with clearer thinking. A pottery class could somehow contribute to sparking a new business idea. A kayaking trip could stimulate confidence to be more adventurous in your career choices.

After years of watching this process unfold, I now tell clients that clarity may come in non-linear ways. Ideas emerge while taking a shower. A vision might even come in a dream. It's as if we are awakening something. And that's achieved most effectively with a multi-sensory blend. It's more fun that way, as well.

Where Marketing Meets Metaphysics

Prior to coaching, I spent more than a decade doing strategic planning in the marketing arena. Several years after leaving that profession, I had been practicing metaphysical and psychic approaches to making decisions. I studied the law of attraction, which suggests that the vibration of our emotions and thoughts draw things to us, like a magnetic force. When it came to a marketing plan for my own business, I almost felt guilty about going back to "old methods." At times I felt like I should just consult with my spirit guides and "live in the now." Happily, I developed a business plan that blended the best of both worlds.

Several pages are on the "mystical" side. My plan includes an opening blessing, guiding beliefs, and an encouraging letter from my Angel team. There's a holistic checklist of fuel for my mission. This includes things like meditative yoga and walks in nature to seek inspiration and renew my zeal for the work ahead. And a section labeled "Expressing the Mission" includes more traditional elements such as a situation analysis, target audience profiles, measurable goals, strategies and tactics, budget and calendar schedules. I really wanted to live the blend. I also had fun creating an acronym to help me transform my understanding of the word "plan." The cover page reads, "Marian's passionate new P.L.A.N: Purposefully Living with Abundance in the Now.

Seeking the Middle Path

Part of what I love about my life these days is a combo platter that features both "finding my true spiritual path" *and* ambition and achievement. I'm not suggesting a wacky caricature that's half monk, half corporate mogul. It's more integrated. The spiritual foundation motivates me to achieve, to be in service to an inspiring mission. We could call it spiritual ambition. Also, I'm learning another level of that middle ground that makes life more interesting. Beyond right and wrong lies what feels true. Instead of us-versus-them we can look for our common human and spiritual connections. We can genuinely seek win-win rather than taking sides. Between the passive, accommodating, nice girl and the selfish power-climber is the chance to be assertive with grace. Blending the best of both worlds is a highly rewarding way of co-creating with all of your resources. To fuel the joyful blend we are all seeking, we look to the next chapter, and what I call the Three Layers of Inspired Living.

chapter three

The Three Layers of Inspired Living

Change is
  inevitable.
Growth
  is intentional.

Glenda Cloud

The Three Layers of Inspired Living

Can you imagine yourself feeling supported and guided by a magical surfboard while actively creating the inspired life you deserve? Over the years, I've become a fascinated student of what it takes to empower and guide that adventure. Just to summarize a bit, we've established that "Having a plan is not the answer," and asked what besides a plan *does* lead to inspired lives. We also started to gently probe the significant question of "Who am I meant to be?" We have discovered that the either/or tug of war between "finding your true spiritual path" or "ambitiously succeeding in the real world" is delightfully replaceable with your own custom *blend*. To help you build a strong foundation for achieving this blend, let's look at the three layers of inspired living. I just want to briefly introduce the concepts here, and then we'll expand on each in the following pages.

Layer I: Awareness- Responsibility-Choice

Deeper awareness is essential for any kind of constructive growth. One simple, yet powerful model to help you experience inspired living is an intentional cycle of Awareness-Responsibility-Choice. This productive, informed cycle becomes the engine that moves you through life.

Layer II: Your Compelling Charter

In order to make effective choices in sync with your authentic self, you need a Compelling Charter comprised of meaningful Values, Purpose and Vision. These infuse your Planning and Choices, as you navigate through a more conscious, intentional life experience.

Layer III: Mind-Body-Spirit Fuel

You want your Compelling Charter to emanate from sources of

inspiration beyond just your clever brain. By going deeper into your body and spirit, and proactively incorporating this into your life habits, you are better equipped to make truly inspired choices. Paying attention to Mind-Body-Spirit vitality also gives you greater energy, fueling your capacity to continue waking up inspired and falling asleep grateful.

3 Layers of INSPIRED LIVING

Layer I*

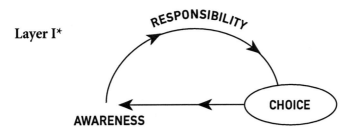

*The ARC of Inspired Living

The ARC of Inspired Living:
Awareness- Responsibility- Choice

Too often, our culture promotes an ethos of pushing to make things happen and living on fast-forward. Rarely tuning in to what's going on *inside*, we may get caught up in unconscious, auto-pilot patterns that lead to angst and, ultimately, regret. How do we shift to a more rewarding, meaningful existence? We replace the less conscious patterns with an intentional, ongoing cycle of Awareness-Responsibility-Choice. In this cycle, you remain deeply aware of "who you are," what you earnestly want to fuel, and what's actually happening day to day. You remember that you are responsible for creating your own well being and success. Coming from heightened *awareness* and *responsibility*, you make conscious *choices* that are more in tune with your true spirit. Each choice gives you a consequence and evokes certain feelings, and thus new learning feeds back into awareness. This conscious cycle leads to feeling more alive and grateful for the adventure. Life starts to flow.

The first time you digest this information, it may sound like an academic formula. Rest assured that it quickly becomes a natural habit. One of my former clients emailed to rejoice about how her life was turning out, with work she loved and a new romance brewing. She kept a small note with "Awareness-Responsibility-Choice" taped to her bathroom mirror. She was delighted to report how this was paying off in real life.

Awareness

Awareness is paramount. If you have the ability to pause and "check in" with your core values, authentic priorities and inner wisdom, and then relate these to your daily living, you are tapping into true inspiration. Being awake and alert, you can no longer be snoozing through your own spin cycle.

Renewed awareness often begins with observations of your external world- your environment, circumstances, relationships, and other relevant data-gathering for heightened clarity. You want to become an observer and student of your life. You seek to gain insights about patterns and your natural processes. You are focused on what works for you and what doesn't, so that you keep gaining mastery in managing your life energy.

You'll also want to cultivate a keen awareness of your inner world- your feelings, what drives you, your beliefs, your desires, your intuition and ongoing inner guidance. As you increase your knowledge of who you are and who you truly feel called to be, you'll notice how well this awareness aligns itself with your day-to-day activities. As you integrate the ARC of Inspired Living practices into your own life habits, you'll begin to achieve harmony between your inner intelligence and how you operate in real life. That harmony is what stimulates joy and awakens all kinds of new possibilities.

A very important cousin to awareness is self-acknowledgement: the ability to stop, notice and celebrate your own growth and accomplishments. Because celebration of the individual for its own sake is typically not encouraged past grade school, I emphasize this with my coaching clients. We often start sessions with "celebrations" of events, choices, or moments of awareness from the previous week. As an example, Rick celebrated that he caught himself being less sarcastic at work and consciously choosing to be more compassionate at home. Tina celebrated the completion of a professional training program and acknowledged the perseverance it took. Joan celebrated feeling more aware of what we called her "capacity management" in a prior session. She celebrated that she had gained confidence in creating more breathing room. We each need to develop the capacity to be our own best advocate - to acknowledge that we are pleased and proud of who we are becoming.

If awareness starts with *know thyself*, it must end in knowing how you are making an impact on your environment. How well do you perceive how others may feel about what you have said or done? How aware are you of how your presence influences a situation? Profound awareness includes awareness of what's going on within you, around you, how you are connected to others, the impact you bring about, and your ability to pay attention to all of it. If we assigned weighted percentages to the Awareness-Responsibility-Choice cycle, awareness could fill about 80 to 90%.

The next tool, called Spy on Yourself, will help you cultivate the ability to increase your awareness. Have fun with this. You'll find that this simple awareness tracking practice can lead to breakthroughs in your perspectives and behaviors.

For about one week, pause and Spy on Yourself once or twice a day. In a Spy on Yourself moment, you're simply checking in, like a temperature check of your feelings or other aspects of self-awareness. Do your best to not judge yourself. Don't worry about making changes at first. The intention is merely to observe and become more aware.

Here's a menu of ways to Spy on Yourself. Select one focus from the examples below, or let these inspire your own custom check-in question.

How am I feeling about being "in sync with my true spirit"? When or how do I experience disharmony between my inner values or desires and my outer experience?

How satisfied am I with how I am investing my energy? What could I tweak to feel more fulfilled and productive?

What do I notice about feeling authentic or speaking my truth (versus pretending, stuffing down feelings or requests, etc.)?

Use a Spy on Yourself moment to acknowledge your efforts, accomplishments and growth in awareness, e.g. "I can celebrate that I'm not rushing around on auto-pilot today. I am noticing what could inspire me and beginning to think about how to create more of that in my life."

A favorite use of this tool among my clients is tracking Energizers and Drainers. In your notebook, simply create two columns labeled "Energizers" and "Drainers." Jot down your insights each day for at least a week. This is a great awareness tracking tool to help you make room for more fulfillment, less drag. After enough data gathering, ask "How will I enhance or expand the Energizers?" and "How will I delegate, diminish or dump the Drainers?" Of course, we can't simply remove all of our Drainers, but we can get creative about how to respond to them.

Each of these could be the focus of a brief, private check-in. It's often helpful to set up a beeper or computer pop-up to remind you to check in and jot down your observations. Remember, just notice and gather data. As you increase your attentiveness over time, this allows your natural growth instincts to kick in. Your awareness alone will plant seeds within you to guide more conscious choices.

Responsibility

As someone who cares wholeheartedly about your options for Inspired Living, I have good news and bad news. The good news is that you absolutely can create the life you want. The bad news? *You* must create the life you want. You alone have the power to do this. It can't be done for you, plopped in your lap, or be handed down from the clouds. Of course, this really isn't bad news at all. Accepting responsibility means you're in the driver's seat. Real success and soul satisfaction are generated from your responses, from the inside out.

The R in the ARC is about remembering that each of us is responsible for creating our own well being and success. You don't need to feel intimidated by responsibility. Rather than associate responsibility with a sense of obligation or burden, you can view it as a source of freedom. Consider what is within your power or influence. Let's play with that for a moment. Ask yourself sincerely, "What is within my power?" I may not control the weather, other people, external circumstances and other facts of reality, but I do have the power to choose how I respond to everything I encounter. I can create my own "inner weather" on a rainy day. I can remember that I need not be a supporting actor in someone else's drama. Harder to swallow, but still the truth: I have the power to accept responsibility for my own feelings of sadness, anger, frustration, etc. and not play the victim role, crying, "They made me feel…" I also have power and responsibility for how I behave, what I say, even what I think and how I talk to myself. I am responsible for who I am, who I am becoming, and how I show up every day. How could anyone else possibly be in control of this? It's a fascinating torture that we inflict on ourselves to believe otherwise.

In the movie *Parenthood*, Steve Martin's character has worked up a lather of frustration, trying to juggle his boss' relentless demands for performance and pressure to spend more time with his emotionally sensitive son. This pressure is made all the worse by his brother-in-law's constant pontification on brilliant child-development techniques. When his wife asks, "Do you have to?" about something, Martin's character explodes, lamenting, "My whole life is *have to!*"

We've all felt this way to some degree. It makes you want to hug him, or say, "Yeah, let's go have a beer…" Of course, we want to have compassion in these moments. It's natural to feel frustrated and trapped by mortgage payments, demanding jobs, families and too many to-do lists. However, what happens when we fall into the mode of blaming our circumstances or other people? We give away our personal power. The truth is that each of us has the capacity to establish our own standards, boundaries, goals, beliefs and actions that will lead to a life we feel grateful for, rather than a life that we endure.

There are other higher levels of responsibility as well, such as our responsibility to each other as a community, or using our power wisely—through love and service rather than manipulation and greed. For now, let's just focus on the basic principle of taking responsibility for creating your own well-being and success. This means becoming more mindful of slipping into the victim trap, or holding others responsible for your life condition. When we react out of ego-driven fears we end up sabotaging ourselves. Keep in mind your ability to respond. You can always attempt to contribute to your highest good. Remember that you are an *active participant*, co-creating with the flow of life energy within and all around you.

I have come to appreciate responsibility as a gift, a privilege. Once upon a time I was diagnosed with a disease and told I would suffer with this for the rest of my life. Back then, I couldn't grasp that I didn't have to accept exactly what some doctors told me. I didn't fully appreciate that I could take charge of my health, my career course, or anything else I really wanted to. Now I know that I can take responsibility for creating a new story for my life. I *get to* make new choices. That's why, in a nutshell, responsibility is about reclaiming your genuine power to *create* your life. It has been possible for me and it is possible for you.

• • • Reflect on Your Response-ability • • •

Take a moment to reflect on your own ability to create *your* responses.

We all slip into feeling victimized by external circumstances at times. How might you give away your power?

What would help you to reclaim your power for creating your own experiences?

Think of a situation that may feel heavy or draining. What is *not* your responsibility? (Hint: other people's choices, reactions, and things you just can't control, etc.) What *is* your responsibility? How could you tweak *who you are being* in this context to feel less drained? How might you learn or grow from this experience?

Choice

We all know what it's like to feel overwhelmed. At workshops I have led for professional women the participants reveal yearnings for a more meaningful, rewarding or just easier life. They admit to feeling like they are often on autopilot, always running and letting their lifestyles run them. In a brave moment of candor, they agree with my challenge that no one is holding a gun to their heads to continue this way. In that moment, they find themselves at the brink of realizing that their entire life condition stems from a series of choices.

This insight can be the beginning of your very own revolution. The perspective that there are no "have to's" and that "everything is a choice" can be hard to swallow. Even as you read this, you may be thinking, "Oh, Marian, that's too idealistic. You just don't get what my life is really like."

What's useful at this point is the realization that you can take each "I have to..." statement and replace it with "I choose to..." This is both annoying and freeing, depending on the mood, timing and context of this news flash. Believe me, my husband has caught me in frustrated moments, griping, "I have to..." about something. He'll insert, "You mean you *choose* to?" with a sheepish grin. "Yeah, yeah, I choose to," I'll retort, knowing that I deserve a good dose of my own dogma.

Yes, realizing that we are *always at choice* can be both empowering and exasperating. I assure you that you are much better off fully embracing "everything is a choice" as a gift rather than viewing this as a burden. Your first choice is this: Do you want to be a victim of circumstance or a creative chooser?

Another fundamental touchstone for your choices comes from your beliefs or perspectives. Will you choose to come from possibility or from limitation? Take a moment and recall when you have heard yourself or others say, "I'm not very good at relationships" or "I'm always lousy at speaking to groups" or "He'll be defensive if I...." These tiny phrases (with huge consequences) are all choices we make.

I overheard a woman say to her friend, "I know I'm not a lucky person..." This is not an objective truth. She has *chosen* to believe this. Guess what she'll continue to create? She'll generate more "proof" that she is unlucky and the nasty, self-defeating cycle will continue, until she makes another choice. I'm not suggesting that by simply choosing something, it is so. I could say, "I choose to be a famous tennis player" yet not have the natural talent or likelihood to develop that skill. On the other hand, I do assert that fueling beliefs such as, "I choose to be vitally healthy" or "I choose to create win-win" (rather than assuming someone else won't collaborate) does carry real power.

Please don't hear this as me naively declaring that you get to have your way all the time or that following Awareness-Responsibility-Choice guarantees bliss 24 hours a day. There are trade-offs, sacrifices, tough choices, and compromises to be made. The inspired person makes these choices consciously and deliberately, coming from accepting his or her own finely tuned awareness and response- ability. Choice is not synonymous with fault. If a bus hits you tomorrow, will that be your fault? No. That's ludicrous. However, I would say that you could accept responsibility for how you respond to this experience. How you manage your own thoughts, beliefs, emotions and behaviors is your choice.

The longer I coach people, the more I believe this simple ARC formula has high potential for equipping them to create extraordinary lives. Beyond any one specific "result" outcome, I want clients and Wake Up Inspired readers to create personal joy and good works in the world because they are effectively practicing Awareness- Responsibility- Choice.

Pardon the cliché, but this is also very much about "Success is a journey, not a destination." It would be a mistake to let coaching (and working with this book) become focused only on fixing problems and concocting projects. It's not as simple as you have a dream, so you devise a plan to go achieve that, and voila! Another slippery slope might be, "Once I have that or become this, then I'll be truly fulfilled." There's nothing terribly wrong with this, except that life just doesn't work that way. Your more bountiful treasure lies in your ability to manage an ongoing series of choices for the rest of your life. The ARC is a way of perceiving, learning and living that can absolutely become a natural habit. It's like the parable of giving a man a fish so that he may eat for one day or teaching him to fish so that he may enjoy the fruits of a good, long life.

• • • • Reflect on the Gift of Choice • • • •

How might you view (awareness-and-responsibility-fueled) choice as a gift? What would feel *lighter*? What would encourage you to move forward with positive energy?

Try listing some of your "I have to....." sentiments and replace these opening words with "I choose to..." Explore how you could come to embrace them as true choices.

As an example, a client, Alison, feels obligated to attend a volunteer committee meeting. This is understandable, of course. Yet the truth is she has options, including canceling or not showing up. Alison can say to herself: *I'm aware that I'm tired and don't really feel like going. I'm also aware that I agreed to participate and that I highly value commitment. I take responsibility for weighing the possible consequences and benefits of my options. I don't want to be driven by duty or guilt. I do wish to be inspired by my inner guidance and core values. Ultimately I choose to go, because my logical brain, my heart and my gut wisdom align to tell me that's the true choice in this moment.* On other nights, Alison might choose to cancel for the sake of another compelling priority, or to practice what I call proactive resentment prevention. That means she takes responsibility for managing her well-being and her capacity for continued positive contributions.

Overall, what intrigues *you* about this Awareness-Responsibility-Choice concept so far? What are possible applications to your life?

The Power of Choice

When we come to realize, in the cells of our bodies, that *every thought and every action is a choice*, this frees our souls. It feels uplifting. It feels true. With each true choice we make, our lives can be in alignment with who we truly are. Our choices transform our hearts. Our choices move our feet into real action. Choices change us. Choices change the world.

In the second Harry Potter extravaganza, Professor Dumbledore has a pivotal conversation with Harry near the film's end. The young wizard is concerned, if not a bit frightened, by his abilities and their possible inner link to darker forces. In a way, he's asking his grand sage to tell him if he's actually a good boy or maybe a bad boy fooling everyone, including himself. "It is not our abilities that make us who we are, Harry. It is our *choices*," Dumbledore assures him.

Indeed, it is our choices that shape our beliefs, our experiences, our chances for fulfillment, and living up to our soul's path. There's a quick litmus test I sometimes use as a shortcut to discerning a true choice. It's as if a quiet strength within asks, "What choice would have you feeling taller? What choice would have you feeling smaller?" Try this the next time you'd like a little boost of clarity. We have countless opportunities to feel taller or smaller spiritually, mentally, and emotionally every day of our lives. What are your choices? Fear or love? Judgment or compassion? Resistance or curiosity? Doubt or faith? Choices are made with inspiration or inertia. You are already choosing everything.

We can also recognize the potential power of collective choice. What if enough people choose to believe that we are creating a hopeful, new world vision together (or conversely, that things are getting worse and worse)? Our chosen perspectives and intentions influence that greater field of collective thought. I encourage you to find joy in realizing that your choices can contribute positive energy not only to your own life, but also to all life.

Now that we have a little added incentive to make thoughtful choices, how do we know we're making choices in sync with our true spirit? One essential element is being grounded in who you are and your authentic priorities. For this, you need to make the most of your inner sense of direction. With long-term, continuous cultivation, your internal navigation system can become a natural, keen sense of tracking. Psychic Sonia Choquette would say "trust your vibes." I have studied with Sonia and love her methods for building intuitive strength. I also recognize that someone like Sonia has been cultivating this trust since childhood, so she's achieved a masterful level of intuition beyond what most of us experience. We could also consider monks who have been meditating for decades. For the rest of us, we have some catching up to do. Tools like Tune In Time (introduced in Chapter 2) are designed to strengthen that connection for you and me. It's also quite helpful to have something we can comprehend and follow with our five senses. One powerful process for this is developing your Compelling Charter. This is the second layer of Inspired Living.

3 Layers of INSPIRED LIVING

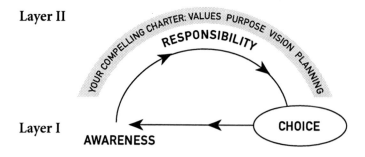

Layer II

YOUR COMPELLING CHARTER: VALUES PURPOSE VISION PLANNING
RESPONSIBILITY

Layer I

AWARENESS   CHOICE

Your Compelling Charter

Many clients say, "Help me to make those wise choices aligned with what I really want to create. Don't let me be seduced by the first opportunity just to be engaged again." It's easy to get excited about a new idea, job offer, relationship, or other invitation from the universe. How do we make choices coming from love versus lack, creativity versus myopia?

By developing your own compelling charter, you can feel more confident in your intentions. Imagine being a good steward of what your true spirit wants to express through you. Consider this as a reference point to help you honor heartfelt promises you make to yourself. The meaning of the word charter includes "special privilege," and qualities such as "majestic" and "potent." So I invite you to infuse your exploration of charter with a sense of privilege and potency.

You Can See Clearly Now: Values, Purpose, Vision, Planning

The formula for your compelling charter is Values, Purpose, Vision, and then Planning and Choices. These fundamental guideposts will fuel inspired choices. Your charter is a way of articulating your deeper inner guidance, helping you to navigate the course. Coming up soon, I'll offer exercises to help you gain insights to develop your own custom-built charter. Please give yourself permission for this to be a great start and not expect to have it all figured out. Exploring your authentic values, purpose and vision should take time, perhaps months of thoughtful curiosity and illumination. We could also say that this process is a lifetime journey, not a quickie exercise we do once and say "got that done." Let this be fun and intriguing. Consider how you might be in a courtship phase, wanting to know all about a new lover or new business client. Embark on learning more about the most important VIP client and personal relationship of your life… that person is you. Enjoy this courtship phase for a while.

It really helps to get your charter expressed in writing. Sharing this process with trusted support partners will help you gain clarity and make it real. You will feel energized to be charting your own authentic course. Keep in mind that you want this to be meaningful, meaty and actually *used* because it motivates you and propels you forward. You don't want this to become pith on paper, forgotten in a journal somewhere.

It's a
funny thing
about life.
If you refuse to
accept anything but the best,
you very often get it.

Somerset Maugham

Your Compelling Charter

Being a Good Steward of the Inspired Life You're Meant to Lead

VALUES   **Your anchor & rudder**
Who you are

PURPOSE   **Your calling & internal compass**
Legacy
Why you are here

VISION   **Your treasure map & outlook**
What you see and intend

PLANNING   **Steering & discerning**
& CHOICES   *How you navigate*

Values: Getting to Know *You*

It seems that from the beginning of civilization, philosophers, playwrights and prophets have been telling us to "Know thyself" and "To thine own self be true" in various ways, from ancient tomes to modern motivational pod casts. Yet, how well have we heeded these fine words? What have you done lately to know yourself more deeply? How much encouragement have you received in your life to "walk to the beat of your own drummer"? Just visit any commuter station on a Monday morning to see how many unique identities are gleefully expressing their highest potential.

Your most important job is to become your true self. If not, you'll eventually suffer pain and regret. It's absolutely possible to create your life, livelihood and leadership in sync with the real you— and joyful prosperity is your reward.

A starting point is a better understanding of your core values. Values are not good or bad, right or wrong. Your values capture *who* you are, your true nature. They can serve as a rudder for your stewardship through life. Values can also be like an anchor, helping you to be grounded and know what you absolutely want to take a stand for.

It's always a quiet thrill to watch clients gain a deeper understanding of values and then witness them discover how this fuels creating a more rewarding life. I met Alice shortly after she had resigned from a job in a field she thought she'd leave forever. We started our work by shining light on what she had been tolerating and what was in the way of her true fulfillment and sustainable success. We then delved into clarifying her core values and how she might create a whole life more in sync with these, including her work. Alice discovered that, rather than finding a new career, her key to waking up inspired was *finding herself.* Alice said that identifying and understanding her core values made all the difference in the world. Integrity was high on her list. As common as this may sound as a typical value, this provided a clarifying insight for her. She came to terms with why she had been so unhappy and *who she needed to be* from that point on. She actually ended up returning to her company, in a position she designed. She was delighted to be making life choices more aligned with her values. When I asked Alice for wisdom to pass on to her kindred spirits out there, she offered, "Figure out who you are, what you want, and don't be afraid to ask for that… or at least work toward getting there."

Another client, Nina, spoke about how connecting with her values "opened a door to me that just wasn't there before. It was especially eye-opening to recognize *freedom* as a core value. I could own this. It felt like permission to be my true self." Several years later, Nina says knowing her authentic values still profoundly guides her life. "Beyond intellectual reasoning, there's more resonance with an inner core. My choices are made based on *Is this me or not me? Is this who I am?*"

Clients use values to sort out all flavors of choices, from whether to have another child to how to approach a business presentation. I've seen grown men tear up during values discovery work, as they experience being heard, seen and appreciated for who they really are. More importantly they see how they can navigate through life more in alignment with this true self, and what that will open up for them.

Let's confirm that "values" does not refer here to morals or obedience to rules. In this exercise, you want to become fascinated with what you intrinsically value and thus what authentically propels you with positive energy or, conversely, what shuts you down. Sparked by my study with Coaches Training Institute and years of coaching, I've witnessed that it's best to sneak up on the subject of discovering values. More direct approaches, such as starting first with circling value words from a prepared list, may lead to selecting what you think you *should* value. Letting your real life experience *reveal* your values is more accurate and meaningful.

Spy on Yourself to Detect Values

You can use the Spy on Yourself game to start collecting clues about your core values. Become a much more active observer of your feelings, thoughts and behaviors for a couple weeks. Essentially, you are "spying" for positive and negative energy charges. Positive feelings indicate a value that is being expressed or honored. Negative energy offers clues that a value is being violated. As you observe yourself, some themes will emerge to indicate what you value.

When Eva spied on her life, she noticed how alive she feels when decorating her Christmas tree. She enjoys going to great lengths to make it stunning, and to entertain her guests in a warm, welcoming environment. Also, Eva would shudder at the suggestion of serving pizza on paper plates. These tell us that Eva values *beauty* and *hospitality*. Spying on Eva's wardrobe and home, we could also say *elegance*. Feeling fulfilled in her volunteer endeavors revealed values of *service* and *commitment*. Noticing how she loved making a business presentation with a ta-daa! feel to it, we included "*wow factor*" on her values list.

Patti noticed how she relished reading Miss Manners in the newspaper and chose the word *graciousness* to capture her underlying value. She came alive while on a steep learning curve in an especially creative work project, so *challenge* and *creative expression* were added to her list. She noticed feeling perturbed when someone wasn't fully engaging with her. She also berated herself for getting distracted too easily. So, *connection* or *being fully present* could be key values.

Marci noticed how important it felt to multi-task while waiting for a computer file to download. She also felt better if she could handle three errands in one trip to one place. As mundane as this may sound, it helped Marci to recognize that *efficiency* was an important value for her. In her work, Marci noticed feeling frustrated when the process of things dragged on. She felt more fulfilled when she could reach a conclusive solution and be acknowledged for the difference she made. Her underlying values include *results, completion, impact,* and *recognition.*

As you observe your positive and negative experiences each day, record clues in your WUI notebook about the values underneath those feelings. Here are some questions to help focus your spying efforts. Start a list of at least 12 values, perhaps adding a couple each day over time.

When do you feel fulfilled or more alive? (So, what is the value underneath that?)

What are your favorite places and why? Consider when you have felt, "Aah, it's great to be here. I feel *right* and even uplifted by being here." When do you feel the opposite (and thus what value is missing or violated)?

What pushes your buttons in a negative way?

Think of people you admire. What is it about them that engenders your admiration?

Your authentic responses to these questions will reveal what matters, what you hold dear and what drives you. Have fun with this process and know that this is one more step toward living in alignment with the joy meant for you.

Purpose: Why You are Here

Your purpose is your calling and internal compass. My first invitation to you is to *listen* for your purpose rather than to produce it. Intimidating words like purpose or mission can lure us into trying too hard to come up with the perfect answers. This is precisely what you don't want to do. If we follow the notion that we are each born with a purpose for our soul in this lifetime, then it is inherently something to be uncovered, not forced. Purpose begins to emerge when we wholeheartedly ask ourselves, "Why am I here?"

I recall that era of my life when I'd find myself awake at 2 a.m., on the edge of the bed, eyes red and head spinning. Some inner committee was hosting wrestling matches between what I felt and how I thought I was supposed to achieve success. *How on earth could I be unhappy? Other people think I have a fabulous life. What was wrong with me? How did I get here? How do I change my life? How am I going to keep paying my Visa bill? Am I ready for that client presentation tomorrow?*

Over time, I created considerable breathing room to clear my head of this inner debate. Hiking in nature, pursuing holistic health, and personal growth work led to a profound shift. Rather than feeling like a victim, staring out the window at two in the morning, moaning, "What on earth am I to do?", my spirit was growing stronger, more heroic and humble all at once. I began asking in a whole new way, "No, really— *What on earth am I to do*?" I was open for guidance from my higher self in a way than I had never allowed before. The fog began to clear, allowing hope and enthusiasm to come in.

During a workshop, I came up with a core purpose statement: "I am the messenger that invites others to find their own song and choose to follow that music." This was fine for a while, but then a bit soft for the person I was becoming. After coaching for a few years, I did another visualization exercise. I saw myself at a microphone yelling "Wake up!" This made me laugh, because that's not quite my style in real life. I also knew that this spoke to the essence of my purpose - something about helping others to wake up and not miss out on the amazing lives they could have. In this exercise, we wanted to find something symbolic of "not letting people sleep." I thought of the early morning honking horns in my neighborhood, for people being picked up for school and work. (Which I find rude, but sure gets my attention.) This led to a new core purpose statement: "I am the honking horn that will not let you be asleep to your true spirit."

This purpose statement has stuck. It informs who I am and how I show up every day in a natural, yet uplifting, don't-get-too-complacent way. (Of course I don't want to be rude, but this does inspire me to be lovingly feisty about encouraging others to not settle.) A few years after establishing this purpose statement, I started teaching and writing with the title "Wake Up Inspired." Those words came to me in the wee hours of the morning. I scribbled them down and was pleasantly surprised to find it available as a website URL. I felt excited about the expansion of this aspect of my work. Much later, it hit me that the visualization from several years earlier was prophetic. I honestly had never seen the connection between that image of me saying "Wake up!" and the Wake Up Inspired work. This time, it made me cry with deep gratitude for feeling on path with my divine purpose. That's the potential power of getting curious about your *own* purpose.

It's crucial to realize that your purpose is *not* synonymous with what you do for a living. Don't work yourself into a corner trying to squeeze life purpose into a job. Your purpose is more about *why* you are here in this lifetime and the essence of the contributions you bring to life, rather than the context of what you are doing. Yes, my core purpose statement fits perfectly with my work. However, I could also be a CEO, a nanny, a songwriter, or the manager of a burger joint, and still be living out this purpose. Clients have called me asking questions like, "Which job should I take? Which one matches my purpose best?" The most useful response is, "How will you bring your purpose to whichever job you choose?"

So many of us seem to struggle with wanting to "find ourselves" and go searching on the internet for the position or place out there that will give us wealth and contentment, so that we'll feel like we have found our purpose. My suggestion: Stop looking *out there.* Your higher purpose stems from an urge to serve rather than a drive to get more recognition, stuff, or whatever our ego fools us into craving. So when it feels right to explore this further, ease your body back, relax your shoulders, and listen with your heart for what you are called to *give.*

• • • • Peek at Purpose • • • •

Let's have fun with three trips through time and space to uncover insights about your purpose. Don't try hard to develop a grandiose purpose statement. Relax and let the following visualizations be filled with childlike curiosity. It's also smart to warm up your state of mind for this exercise. Try breathing, stretching, and moving gently to music with your eyes closed to set the stage for letting your imagination, memories, and insights flow.

You are about to envision three places. (This is a bit like the three Spirits that visit Ebenezer Scrooge in *A Christmas Carol,* without any scary parts.) Get your notebook ready to capture a few insights after each "trip."

Trip 1: Revisit your 90th birthday party.

Close your eyes and return to your 90th birthday party (introduced in Chapter One). This time, especially notice what's creating joy for your future self relevant to the *impact* she has had on other people. What do others say or feel about the difference she has made in their lives? Notice the essence of the contribution she has made in her lifetime. What do you observe? Imagine that 90-year-old smiling at you and offering you a bit of wisdom about who you are meant to be. Listen with your heart. When you feel ready, open your eyes and jot down whatever comes to you in your notebook.

Trip 2: Visit your 9ᵗʰ year.

The second trip is a glimpse from your life at age 9 (or some time in childhood that you are drawn to). Close your eyes and let yourself be transported back to a memory of when you felt alive, at your best and fulfilled. What did you love to do? What were some of your innate qualities, interests and talents? When you've gathered enough information from this trip, open your eyes and write in your notebook.

Trip 3: Peek in on people you admire.

Building on the previous Values exercise, note a few people you admire. (They can be living or dead, people you know, or admired from afar. They can be characters from a book, movie or play.) Close your eyes for a moment to understand why you admire them, perhaps seeing them in your mind's eye. Focus on the qualities that most resonate with you. Write these qualities in your notebook.

Drafting Your Purpose Statement

Each of these trips offers clues to help you connect to who you are meant to be.

In your notebook, play with adding to the following preface: "I am meant to _____" based on some of these clues. Here's an example to help inspire you.

Imagining her 90ᵗʰ birthday party revealed to Mia that she's meant to bring out the best in others, with optimism and humor. She saw her 90-year-old self as a person with an easy smile that helped others gain confidence. (You see how these are core "gifts" or roles that could be applied to many contexts, rather than one specific career description. Purpose is found in who you are *being* more than what you are doing.)

Childhood memories revealed to Mia that she loved to play dress up, sing, and dance for family and friends. She loved playing with a big piece of fabric to create several unique gowns, and put on little fashion shows. Her family teased her about being a bit of a ham, using kitchen spoons or drapery cords as microphones. Mia laughed while recalling this, and realized that she is meant to be creative and to have some sense of performing (or presenting) in her life.

Let's continue with Mia and the qualities of people she admired.

Admire	Why? / Qualities
Grandmother	Gutsy. Spirit-fueled. Loving, bold teacher. Fun and substance integrated.
Dr. Malcolm Sayer in the movie, *Awakenings* (played by Robin Williams)	Determined, fueled by loving, learing, helping, healing motives. Made the best of non-ideal opportunity and circumstances. Really smart. Kind.
Maya Angelou	Beautiful stories, prose/language. Powerful presence. No B.S., calling-us-forth inspiring. Insightful, wise teacher. Gracefully proud.

A fascinating glimpse at your purpose can be found in those qualities that you admire in others. This offers clues about the qualities you are meant to embody and express. Using the above examples from Mia, we could select a few qualities and add the preface, "I am meant to ..." as follows:

A) I am meant to be a gutsy, loving teacher, bringing out the best in others with fun and substance.

or

B) I am meant to tell beautiful stories that help people learn and heal.

Note that version A incorporates the "bringing out the best in others" that came from her 90th birthday party visit. We can see Mia's creativity and sense of performing (from her childhood memories) having room for expression in both of these purpose statements.

Your Turn

Write "I am meant to …." and let some thoughts flow, inspired by the three trips. Don't worry if your notes are too long or too short or whatever. This will lead to drafting a purpose statement. Let these exercises be like getting pregnant with insights about your purpose. Don't push to have the final answer. Have fun. Then let it go. We'll come back to using purpose once more, later in the book.

To Give or Not to Give

Let's bring up an important precaution about discovering purpose and joy in what you give. You need to be especially cognizant about the condition of your energy before "doing for others." Seeker-Achiever women have an intuitive sense of giving and helping embedded in their destiny. The problem is that too many of us get stuck trying to please and perform for clients, bosses, family, partners and friends. It's hard not to identify with these roles and accomplishments. At times, we may even be unintentionally earning martyr badges on our grownup Girl Scout sashes. This kind of striving stems from what could be called a "lower energy vibration," as if we need to prove something or earn our worthiness. If this resonates with you, you need to stop giving at that level, and make self-love a priority for a while. You also need to evaluate what's been driving the previous behavior. Only after a deeper connection to your higher self and your true choices can you pursue *doing for others* in healthier, more rewarding ways. It needs to come from a pull, a heart's desire that catches fire. When you feel that "higher energy vibration" in your giving—more inspiration than drive - and then give it your all, you will experience your utmost joy.

Listening to your heart,
finding out
who you are,
is not simple.

It takes time
for the chatter
to quiet down.
In the silence of "not doing"
we begin
to know what we feel.

If we listen and hear
what is being offered,
then anything in life
can be our guide.

Listen.

Source unknown

Vision: Seeing Where You Want to Go

One of my favorite lines came from this Japanese proverb, shared by a client; "Vision without action is a daydream. Action without vision is a nightmare." Even when we think we have a vision, that image might not be sharp enough. Vagueness can be an insidious form of self sabotage. You want your vision to capture what it *looks like* to have your values and purpose being expressed in real action, at a certain point in time. Vision is about what you see and intend.

Imagine you're standing at the bow of your ship, wind in your hair, feeling heartened by your renewed sense of purpose. Something like "My purpose is to remind others that they can fly" is coursing through your veins (or replace this with your own gung-ho purpose). Just for fun, see yourself like Barbara Streisand in the movie *Funny Girl*, at the bow of the boat, hands on the rail, belting out, *Get ready for me love cuz I'm a comer. I simply gotta march, my heart's a drummer. Don't bring around a cloud to rain on my parade.* At some point, one of the crew taps you on the shoulder and asks, "Excuse me lady, but where do you want us to go?...Can you show us a picture or a map or something so we know where to dock this baby for a while?" We need to *name* our heart's desires. To point and say, that's what I want. That's where I'm headed.

You don't need to rush into claiming your vision. Another form of subtle sabotage is our own impatience. Clients come into coaching understandably anxious to jump into action and create results right away (especially with career transition). Just as with purpose, you want to tune in and *allow* your vision to emerge rather than manufacture it too quickly. It can make all the difference in the world to know what you really want, and more importantly, what will truly serve you well, before diving in.

Consider marching down the aisles of the supermarket with an empty, growling stomach, without any specified grocery list.

What will end up in your cart? Life-enhancing choices, or over-priced, quick gratifications? Substandard items bought because of fatigue and hunger? Conversely, imagine creating your shopping list after you've examined your physical, mental, emotional and spiritual needs, and assessed your heartfelt priorities. Consider developing a vision as having a thoughtful, *inspired* shopping list of what you deserve and intend to create.

Speaking of not rushing, I won't ask you to do any specific exercise about vision right now. Later on in the book there will be a section devoted to your vision work (in the previously mentioned Life Fitness Trail). For now, let's continue with the final component of your charter.

Listen for the
voices of
your visions;
they are
nearby.

Ntozake Shange

Planning & Choices: The "ING" of Your Life

I'm assuming that you've been exposed to Time Management 101 and useful, linear planning systems. My intention here is to highlight practices for achieving that blend of traditional logic with non-linear, metaphysical principles. This starts with a rather significant epiphany about three little letters. I had been using this "Values, Purpose, Plan" charter with clients for a while when I realized it needed a crucial edit. It was essential to add "ing." The change from "Plan" to "Planning & Choices" is a huge distinction. While we're out there flowing with Awareness-Responsibility-Choice, sometimes we miss the mark, learn, and try again with another choice. There's forgiveness and flexibility built into this perspective. I am not saying don't plan. I am saying embrace the "ING" of your life: be ever open to new choices and your agility to respond to life's curve balls.

There is another compelling reason for staying open and curious. You want to leave room for divine mystery and magic. What does your true spirit want for you? What is meant for you in the grand scheme you can't possibly see? This helps us to remember that our plans may be too small for the life that wants to live through us. You want to leave room for inspirations, unforeseen spiritual nudges, and divine synchronicities. You can enjoy those unexpected twirls and dips (that you didn't even know you could do)!

I have come to live in a way that trusts I am lovingly held by a greater energy field. I am co-creating with that energy at the same time. This may sound rather "woo-woo" but it's actually quite practical and efficient. An enjoyable, productive life requires fluidity rather than rigid attachment to a specific outcome or schedule.

The other day, a colleague was scheduled to come to my office. When she didn't show, and I found her email explaining that she was ill, I thought, "OK, I guess my Angel Team really wants me to be alone today, to write." While I was writing, a desk clock fell to the floor with a loud noise, causing me to turn and wonder how that happened, since nothing had visibly touched it. I smiled and wondered if it was time for me to stop or at least take a break.

The waitress at lunch brought hot tea instead of iced. My intuition told me this was better for my body's digestion than the iced tea I had ordered without much thought.

When a big project fell through a few years ago, my ego crashed, but my subtle sixth-sensory vibe told me that it was all for the best, and destiny held something richer for me in the long run. Later on, I could see that the big project would have been a counterproductive distraction. I can be curious about things falling through (or things falling off my desk) in ways that make me trust in divine order and feel grateful for an invisible support system.

You may think of this as mystical or silly. I choose to incorporate these perspectives because it's a more intriguing, fun and fruitful way to co-create my life. We could call this going with the flow, but let's be clear that it's not the same as being rudderless or letting life bounce you around like a rubber ball. I would have no problem requesting the iced tea, or "trying harder" to succeed with a project if that's what my inner guidance was clearly urging me to do. You want to be firmly rooted in your values, purpose and vision, while always allowing a fluid stream of choices as it all plays out in real life. Things that used to upset me have increasingly lost their drama over time. I used to let resistance or jumping to conclusions spoil my mood and effectiveness. Now, that underlying belief in divine order informs my responses, allowing a calmer state of grace and efficiency to rule the day. Of course I still get upset and impatient, but this fluid way of dancing with life is becoming habit more and more.

Let the ING of life also apply to how you assess your accomplishments. Growth is not linear, like a steep, straight line on a progress chart. Your real life has many back steps, twists and turns. Each of us is always a work in progress. Rather than judging yourself (and others) about how you should have mastered some knowledge or behavior, or gotten over some past wound by now, focus on continuous movement. We are continually learn*ing*, grow*ing*, evolv*ing*.

• • • Choosing Fluidity over Frustration • • •

Consider this as an experiment. Consciously spend a few days being open to trusting that "everything happens for a reason." When things don't go according to your agenda, pause and notice your response options. If this works for you, imagine you have an Angel team (or some sort of higher support) helping to orchestrate the day, giving you opportunities to make choices.

As an example, let's say a person does not show up for a scheduled meeting with you. It's natural to experience disappointment, worry or anger. Have compassion for yourself with these normal human feelings in that initial reaction. It's the next moment that really counts. Now you can practice Awareness-Responsibility-Choice to your advantage. What is the best perspective with which to view this person not showing for your meeting?

Assume that the universe is friendly and wants you to flourish and enjoy your life. How might your "invisible support team" be trying to help you? What is your next best investment of energy?

Continue playing with this idea of choosing fluidity over frustration. Jot down insights and discuss what you are discovering with an open-minded support buddy. What has this experiment taught you? What beliefs or habits would serve you well moving forward? Write about your discoveries and new intentions in your WUI notebook.

We cannot
direct the wind,
but we can adjust
our sails.
Bertha Calloway

Tapping into Your Mind-Body-Spirit Fuel

Paradoxically, part of what gives you the buoyancy to stay fluid with your planning and choices is that you feel solidly grounded in your charter. Simply put, the more you trust the veracity of your values, purpose and vision, and attempt to create a life in harmony with these, the more fulfilled you will be. So, it's imperative that the impetus for your charter come from your belly and your heart, not just your head.

The third layer of Inspired Living is the ever-essential Mind-Body-Spirit Fuel. We keep throwing around the phrase "mind-body-spirit" and get desensitized to its significance. The words "mind-body-spirit" are liberally used for shampoo label copy and ad campaigns for expensive cruises. For our inspired lives to actually flourish, we need to roll up our sleeves and deeply explore what our own mind-body-spirit integration is all about. Tapping into the energy and wisdom from your body and spirit is like discovering a wellspring of inspiration. When we awaken all of our resources- especially reconnecting below the neck, we find our groove.

3 Layers of INSPIRED LIVING

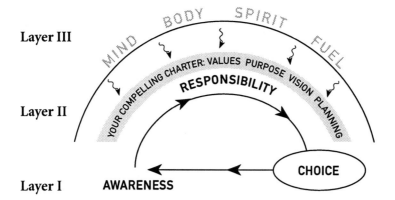

Using More Than Your Head

During my semi-conscious, overdrive era, my inner spirit started knocking, "Can we TALK?" In the meantime my body developed endometriosis, a supposedly incurable disease that added chronic pain, nausea and infertility to the agenda. My sister sent me *Women's Bodies, Women's Wisdom* by Dr. Christiane Northrup. One paragraph virtually changed my life. In essence it said that endometriosis is the illness of competition. From a metaphysical perspective, it is a woman's body telling her that the way she's driving herself relentlessly in the outer world is competing with her innermost needs and true nature.

What some doctors had viewed as only a structural, physical problem was revealed to me in a whole new light. I had been convinced I had to get my health fixed "here" and only then go deal with my career and the rest of my life "over there." It became powerfully clear that these were never separate entities. My physical health, career, lifestyle habits, and spiritual and emotional health were all inextricably interrelated. I needed to deal with mind-body-spirit at once, and then I would find healing, sanity, and a paycheck in a balanced package. The message of this paragraph resonated like a bell tone in the cells of my body. Although it was painful, it was not depressing. Actually, it was uplifting. I was finally getting to the heart of a problem and knowing that real change was possible. Most importantly, the higher agenda of *being in sync with my true spirit* started to get clearer. That's quite different from finding a new job, new doctor, or new plan.

The Wake Up Inspired program strives to pass on practical tools for developing the meaningful, prosperous lives so many people want but don't know how to create. Frankly, there are a lot of books and programs out there offering that promise. One shortcoming is a structure that works primarily from the neck up, with an intellectual approach that ignores the synergies of mind, body, and spirit working together. We are directed to figure things out with new ways of thinking and organizing. Because a physical disease was one of my catalysts for change, I was focusing on my body and holistic health at the same time I was exploring how to create a more rewarding livelihood and lifestyle. The integration was obvious. Nonetheless, it was still a *"Hey, your peanut butter ended up on my chocolate and this tastes great together!"* epiphany.

In my earlier searching for life renewal and career transition resources, I noticed that *body* wasn't brought into the picture. While everyone was becoming more informed about mind-body-spirit synergies, I didn't find any one source that was really putting that philosophy into practical application. If you went to a career counselor you would not expect her to ask you about your eating habits or request that you join her in some yoga stretching before discussing your professional skills. The acupuncturist would not engage in clarifying your values or ask you how your strategic plan for the new business idea was coming. I remember attending a "dream life" program in which I wrote and presented a new "dream plan" produced in four easy steps. The workshop high wore off in 48 hours. This plan had been pushed out of my busy, clever mind, not really cultivated from my deeper inner core.

Think about your own exploration of callings, legacy and new intentions. Before you start re-designing your life, ask yourself if you want quick answers that come mostly from thinking above the neck, or more deeply rooted inspiration, stemming from your body-mind-spirit guidance? For example, the *Values, Purpose, Vision* building blocks could be forced out of your brain in a 30-minute written drill. This would have some merit. However, the result would not be nearly as motivating or sustainable as a deeper sense of your true Compelling Charter, cultivated while you were reintegrating body, mind and spirit.

The Mind-Body Connection is Not a One-Way Street

Another evident *a-ha* for me was that the mind-body connection flows both ways. Yet often, the focus of many books and courses is only on how our thoughts influence our bodies. The health care profession has been increasingly using practices such as relaxation techniques, visualization and meditation tools to heal physical symptoms. The premise could be diagramed as such:

MIND ----------------> BODY

Thoughts, mental/emotional states   Physical health

Let's look more closely at how our bodies influence our thoughts. Imagine using your body as a *resource* to help you achieve clear thinking and emotional balance. Your body can be an efficient instrument for enlivening your spirit. Psychology professor and author, Robert E. Thayer, Ph. D. has conducted research which explores various ways of shifting one's mood or state of being. Of all the methodologies Dr. Thayer identified as "mood enhancers" - including calling a friend, caffeine, and sugar snacks - what do you suppose proved to be the most effective and reliable way to positively boost mood? Answer: A brisk ten-minute walk.

As I asserted earlier, you have an innate knowing within you that will help guide you to all of your best choices. Your *body energy* is a very strong link to this guidance. Science tells us that we have more than one "brain center." We have millions of active neurons and neurotransmitters in our hearts and "guts." The Institute of HeartMath demonstrates the value of tapping into a measurable *heart intelligence* that functions as an "information processing center" for optimal decision making. You can take in phrases like "gut wisdom" or someone asking, "What does your heart tell you?" with much more confidence.

Dr. Candace Pert, a pioneer in mind-body research that demonstrates how our emotions are held in the cells of our bodies, was formerly a skeptical scientist. An enthusiastic advocate now of integrative medicine, she told a Body & Soul conference audience that, "If you want to do something great for your emotional health, get a full body massage every week." I would add to that sentiment. If you want to have effective decision making, great strategic planning, creative productivity, enhanced interpersonal relations and the like, *get back in your body*. Engage in some sort of body movement that takes you out of your thinking, plotting and pondering head. Walking, stretching, yoga, dancing, bike riding or just about anything that strikes your fancy can be worthwhile. Obviously, attending to your body will reduce stress and contribute to your overall vitality. This influences the quality of the energy you have available to invest in your dreams. Furthermore, tuning in to your *body wisdom*, and following through on those inclinations, is one of the most efficient ways to be in harmony with your true spirit.

BODY ------------------> MIND

Body awareness, movement, body-mind integration

Thoughts, emotions, effective decision making, communications, et al

A successful executive client I worked with, Jill, was in a phase of being very focused and rewarded by her career. That meant that most of our coaching had been supporting her strategic planning work and professional relationships. She started to notice cravings for body movement, but hesitated in making this a coaching topic. To her this craving seemed to fall into the category of "personal self care," which wasn't a front burner priority at the time. However, when we discussed body-mind connections and recognized her body as a *resource* for her work success, it all clicked and made sense to her. It felt right to honor these cravings and talk about "body stuff" in coaching as an integral part of her pursuit of fulfillment and excellence in her career and life.

Jill continues to incorporate her body into her life priorities in new ways. She's created a dramatic transformation in her relationship with nutrition and she's walking more. She's lost 40 pounds and feels lighter in multiple ways, including having the energy and clarity of thought for both professional and personal goals to be realized with less struggle.

The benefits of body-mind integration clearly flow both ways. Your thoughts influence your body. Your body influences your thoughts. Think of your body as a VIP member of your success team for your true purpose guidance, creative capacities, emotional balance, professional effectiveness and life satisfaction.

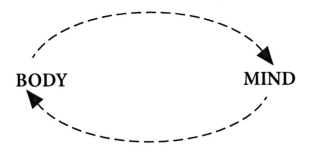

Inspired by examples like my client Jill, I see great value in helping clients avoid making goals "from the neck up." Let's say a new client says that her heart's desire is to experience a rewarding career transition. This is logically perceived as something to be accomplished with greater mental clarity and strategizing. We're also going to explore physical, emotional, and spiritual dimensions to help him or her fuel this dream—not to mention a more rewarding whole life. What I call "optimal energy management" includes body movement, enough sleep, great nutrition, and other forms of mental and emotional nourishment.

This also includes becoming more aware of what feeds your spirit, such as live music or horseback riding. Logically, we could say these "leisure" pursuits compete with the time required to focus on things like preparing for job interviews or writing new business plans. However, fueling yourself with relevant food for your soul will infuse your system with positive energy. This lighter energy contributes to the creativity you will apply to that new business plan. It helps you to show up with more engaging, magnetic energy in important meetings.

To not fully employ *body* and *spirit* would be like managing a project while two-thirds of your workforce just sat at their desks, wondering why you didn't ask them to contribute more. So consider how you could fuel your body and feed your spirit more, then enjoy the return on that investment in other areas of your life.

• • • Hit the Pause Button: Take a Hike • • •

I was invited to be on a panel to address the subject of work-life balance for a MBA alumni club. During the Q&A, someone asked me for advice on how to get started in creating a more balanced life, including a fulfilling career. At the risk of sounding flippant or insulting to my colleagues, I smiled and began my answer, "Take a walk in the woods." Do not belittle this as a quaint thing to do. A good long walk in an inspiring setting can clear out cobwebs and allow you to access your own inner compass. It's certainly a low-cost way to start, as well.

Walking is one of the best ways to Hit the Pause Button. Try a Reboot Walk instead of caffeine fix when you need to jumpstart your afternoon. Consider Mood Walks when you need to shift from cranky to creative. The next time you are bored, stuck or upset, don't stew. Try walking up a fresh mood. Let the first third of your walk be about venting or clearing whatever is bugging you. Then just walk, not really thinking about anything. Breathe and walk briskly, taking in the colors and smells around you. For the last few minutes, focus on the mood you choose to create. Ask yourself what you really want to fuel, and what's not worth your precious energy. I'll bet you can do this whole Mood Walk process in about ten minutes, with practice.

Try on Wisdom Walks with the intention of gaining clarity and momentum. We might say it's walking for the sake of having a meaningful conversation with your higher wisdom. Ideally, a Wisdom Walk is taken in nature, where you can feel that sense of being connected to "Mother Earth" and a greater energy field. In the quiet solitude, you can hear your inner voice more profoundly. However, not all of us have access to this on an average day. Walking down a crowded, noisy, dirty, metropolitan sidewalk is not quite the same as communing with the chirping birds in the woods. Nonetheless, over time, your Wisdom Walk can become a state of being that is not dependant on outside circumstances. It is about going within. With enough inside-out intention and a few environmental helpers, you can start a Wisdom Walk habit fairly easily. Find parks with stretches of green in the middle of urban chaos. Use a headset to filter out the clatter of a busy airport. You can create a Wisdom Walk almost anywhere.

Schedule walking appointments with yourself in your calendar to help you actually make the time. Perhaps you could start with 15 minutes a couple times a week. Build up to 30-45 minutes three or more times per week. If you live near the ocean or a lake, take advantage of the soothing, cleansing powers of water. If walking isn't your thing, you may find other useful ways to allow your inner wisdom to percolate. The most important thing is to cultivate a practice that works well in your life.

If you are seeking
creative ideas,
   go out walking.
Angels whisper to a man
         when he goes
   for a
walk.

Raymond Inmon

Your True Spirit Connection: Within and All Around You

Earlier, we asserted that all of the wisdom and power you need is within you. We need to add another declaration. You are not alone. Your true spirit is one with a collective consciousness. The spirit in you is the spirit in everything. There's that *life force* energy within you and in the sky, the oceans, a leaf in Costa Rica, and the guy sitting next to you on the train. The dance of aliveness happens when you cultivate that "direct line" to your inner spirit hookup and *also* take relevant action. When Spirit calls, you don't let it go into voicemail storage.

By now, you've heard me refer to my Angel Team several times. The screen saver on my computer features Angel images and scrolls with the message, "Marian, you are on the right path and your Angels are helping you." One my favorite ways to cultivate a spiritual connection is to imagine listening for my Angel Team's message for me. Of course I seek guidance on big, meaty decisions. It's also become a way of feeling supported in any moment about anything. This is an intimate relationship, characterized more by "Hey, you guys…" rather than "Oh Great and Mighty …," although I do have immense reverence for this. It's as if there is a group of loving, wise, fun guides serving as my Team. In traffic, I'll say, "OK, Angel Team. I know you're with me, helping us get there safely and on time." If I see an ambulance with lights flashing, I send healing energy and ask my Angels to help those that may be hurt. When the fax machine jams, I affirm their help with the next one going through smoothly. While walking I'll ask for guidance about what to write that day. When I enter a professional conference, I ask my Angel Team to guide me to a chair and trust that I'll be seated next to the person I'm meant to meet that day. When amusing synchronicities happen, I acknowledge them with, "I got it. Very funny." When wonderful things happen, I say "Thank you! Thank you!" It's an ongoing connection, constantly available.

A reasonable question that you may have is, "Marian, are you saying that you are really talking with Angels or that this is part of your vivid imagination?" The bottom line is that I don't know. What if those concepts are not mutually exclusive? I've decided to not get tangled up over what is "real." I just know this works for me. I sense a genuine distinction between my clever ego thoughts and this other energy that comes through. Let me also be clear that I'm not claiming any special abilities to communicate with Angels. I am just like you- a regular Joe tapping into various ways of blending heaven and earth, spiritual and physical planes. Anyone can access the support of their Team, if they so choose.

• • • Tune In To Your Life Support Team • • •

Try to tune in to this energy by writing to yourself from your Team. If Angels don't quite work for you, consider Spirit Guides or an imagined advisory board, cheering squad, or whatever framing feels uplifting and useful. Find a quiet moment, perhaps out of your typical environment. This could be a special place in nature or a nearby library. You can do it anywhere, including the middle of a busy, noisy restaurant. You may have a specific question, or simply be open to whatever messages come through. You could start by writing "Dear Team..." or "Dear Divine Inspiration...," with a brief question such as "What guidance do you have for me today about...?" Take a few breaths, relax and write the response (from your team, to you) "Dear (your name)," and then just let it flow. Over time, a communication flow will grow stronger and faster— like going from dial-up to high-speed. Try it and see what wants to become an inspiring habit for you.

I think my Angel Team habit was enlivened years ago by a beautiful visualization exercise at a workshop with author and teacher Dr. Joan Borysenko. The meditation is called "Invocation of the Angels," and brings in the four archangels for clarity, forgiveness, healing, strength and creativity. Apparently Hollywood cast my visualization, as I couldn't help but see actors like Joe Mantegna (smoking a cigar, no less) and Susan Sarandon as two of the angels. I heartily recommend Dr. Borysenko's audio recording of this ancient meditation (see Resources). I used this daily for a long while, and I'm sure it contributed greatly to various leaps of trust when I had that big lump in my throat. Exercises like this are intended to help you align with your deepest, highest knowing. I encourage you to let that wisdom guide you to become who you are meant to be. It can be unsettling, but it is the most rewarding way to live. You will find your wings more and more.

Finding your wings also takes structure. Now that you know the foundations of Inspired Living, we can bring it all together in one practical application structure—your Inspired Life Fitness Trail. The next section is devoted to giving you a tour of the trail and a healthy taste of the tools you can put to good use in your own life.

In their freedom, birds
make expanding
circles in the sky.
How do they learn to be free?
They fall—and by
falling
are given
wings to fly.

Rumi

SECTION 2

chapter four
Your Inspired Life Fitness Trail

Don't be afraid
of death.
Be afraid
of an
unlived
life.

From Tuck Everlasting

Your Inspired Life Fitness Trail: A Holistic Approach

I believe with all my heart that we need to pursue any mission, transition, or renewal experience with a holistic approach. We need quiet time to awaken our true spirit desires and access our soul's wisdom. To really think straight, we often need to get out of our heads and more into our bodies. Physical exercise also gives us the energy we need to explore our callings. Understanding our emotional motivations and belief patterns helps guide us into right-fit work and relationships. A walk in the sunshine inspires fresh ideas while providing vitamin D, boosting your immune system and preventing disease. Certain foods will influence your clarity or confusion. Donuts impact your dreams (clogging your thinking and your arteries). Body massage stimulates the release of chemicals in your body to promote calm and well being. Influenced by the massage, you'll be in a more receptive state during that challenging discussion with your partner. A slice of reflective solitude at 8 A.M. and healthy eating at noon make the business meeting or art project at 3 P.M. more productive and satisfying. That donut matters. It's all interrelated.

I looked back at what had led to my delicious new life and recognized all of the synergies with added respect and appreciation. I wanted to create a program for others that brought together previously segregated disciplines. The integrative health field touched on "reaching your full potential," yet focused primarily on nutrition, exercise, meditation, and the impact all this has on the cells of your body.

Separately, I found great value in learning more practical structures for vocational and life design approaches. The *plan it- do it* type workshops were fun, but the effects wore off quickly and didn't inspire sustainable shifts. I knew in my deepest core that the mind-body-spirit foundations were what created that sticking power.

Finally, I wanted to be a bridge for bringing the best of mind-body-spirit wholeness to professionals without too much New Agey woo-woo. The early versions of the Wake Up Inspired program began to take shape with long walks, scribbles on napkins, and late nights at the computer. It has evolved through my work with clients over several years.

Imagine that a spiritual director, life and career coach, holistic health advisor, and efficient project manager have all gotten together to design an ongoing optimal program for your inspired life success. That's the spirit of the Life Fitness Trail. A fitness trail is an apt metaphor for this on several levels. You wouldn't do a fitness trail once and say, "I've got it. I'm all done." It's an ongoing process of nurturing new habits and cultivating a way of living. You don't tackle the most difficult exercises right away. You gain competence and confidence over time, especially with the help of a coach or other support system. You fall off course at times, and then get back to walking the talk of the program. It takes patience, self-compassion and perseverance. Also, there's no destination to the Life Fitness Trail circle. In creating the life you really want, there's no final arrival spot either. It's a continuous cycle, evolving like an upward spiral.

In the following pages, you'll see an overview of the trail. There are ten stations on the Inspired Life Fitness Trail, presented in an order that makes sense to me. However, it's worth noting that the way real human beings experience transition and discover a higher mission is not a sequential, chronological process. The true intention of the trail design is for you to gradually assemble a "program" customized for your unique needs, one that will be sustainable and suited to your true nature. Also, you have already seen or done several exercises drawn from the trail in the first three chapters. This voyage is about a reintegration of your whole being. Thus it is inherently and extraordinarily personal. No one can accomplish this feat but you. No one can tell you precisely how to get there.

Inspired Life Fitness Trail

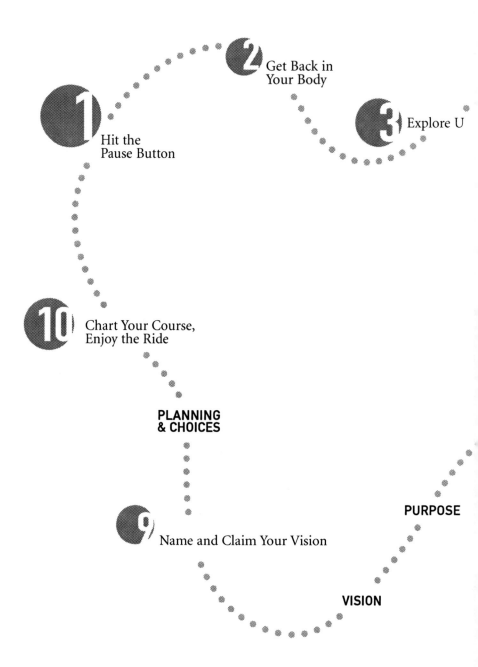

1 Hit the Pause Button

2 Get Back in Your Body

3 Explore U

10 Chart Your Course, Enjoy the Ride

PLANNING & CHOICES

9 Name and Claim Your Vision

PURPOSE

VISION

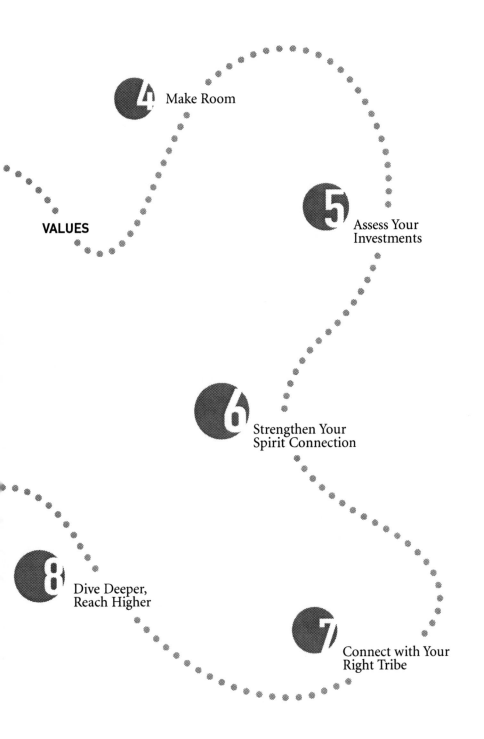

VALUES

Make Room

5 Assess Your Investments

6 Strengthen Your Spirit Connection

8 Dive Deeper, Reach Higher

7 Connect with Your Right Tribe

Before You Hit the Trail…

As mentioned, this book was born out of many Wake Up Inspired workshops and private coaching experiences. Each of the ten stations includes tools that my clients apply over a few months or even years in order to fully integrate them and enjoy the extended results over time. A 400-page course manual was created to offer an extensive menu of tools that clients can select to fit their unique needs and goals. In this next section, I offer some of that menu so that you can get started on your own inspired adventure. For each station, find one or two selected tools to consider applying to your life. Feel free to just scan or skip some of the stations, if you like. Select what appeals to you most for now. You may find that the 13-week schedule supplied in the appendix comes in handy to help with pacing and to keep you from getting overwhelmed. (Remember Lucy and chocolates? Again, be smart about your own capacity and the optimal return on investment of your time and energy.)

Helpful Hints to Set Yourself Up to Succeed:

• **You'll need to *get off the couch*.**

We live in a quick fix, instant-gratification culture. When I see book titles akin to *How to Find Your Soul's Purpose, Get Happy, Rich and Famous in Five minutes* I want to scream. We've all seen those infomercials advertising how you can get washboard abs by wearing some device while lying on the couch eating bonbons. Let me assure you that creating an inspired life requires that you do your own intellectual, emotional, and spiritual sit ups (and some physical exertion as well). In the end you'll be glad you nudged yourself off your comfort zone. The life that's been waiting for you will also rise up to greet you.

• **Don't expect linear progress.**

Don't beat yourself up if it feels at times like you take two steps forward and three steps back. As I've said, my clients are bright, successful achievers. It's natural for all of them to have cycles of creativity and spurts of action, and then experience waves of confusion, doubt, or just needing down time. Rather than punish ourselves for straying from a direct line to a certain goal, we can embrace our process and learn even greater insights about who we are and what works well. We can discern what is a waste of energy – what may feel like *pushing the river*. Strive to honor the intention within each station, whether you follow the specific exercises I suggest or not.

• Go for alignment more than achievement.

It's worth stressing the importance of going for *wholeness* rather than just improving external factors. Your sense of fulfillment from a new job, city or nifty new time management program might not last as long as the thrill of a new hairdo if you don't pursue alignment with your soul. Your outer expression of renewed prosperity may well include things like increased money, professional achievement and a fit body, but these are bonuses, not results-focused obsessions.

• Little things do make a big difference.

When embarking on the pursuit of greater fulfillment, you may expect big dramatic a-has and sweeping change. Yet all of the tiny and mundane investments you make toward creating more inner-outer harmony in your life actually smooth the way for "bigger" insights and tangible opportunities. When life is spinning, you can be too distracted to absorb the tiny moments of happiness available to you. Yet when you're intentionally practicing Inspired Living, renewing mind-body-spirit fuel and making choices aligned with your charter, it feels like the aperture for delight has opened wider. When the blur of an unconscious carousel life is gone, joy comes in on quiet, petite feet several times a day.

• Commit to your own version of Inspired Living.

By experimenting with the ideas and tools at each station, you can begin to chart your very own new adventure. You'll laugh. You'll cry. You'll procrastinate and think some of these things are selfish or a ridiculous waste of time. Then you'll crave the rewarding sensation of your true spirit coming alive. Your soul will wake up and growl, "Feed me!" Ultimately, I hope you will uncover the life you've been looking for (or the self that's been looking for you) and experience the harmony of living in the realm of your own true nature.

The most important hint for succeeding— the secret code of experiencing the most value with these concepts - is *you*. Yes, of course, support from others is essential. Nonetheless, only you can ultimately create the Wake Up Inspired program that will serve you best. Only you can make the commitment and ongoing choices. This collection of tools will provide thought-starters and guidelines for a new path.

The journey is yours to create.

Be patient with yourself, the clock and the calendar.

Have fun exploring!

"I decided to step
off
the road and
cut me
a new
path."

Maya Angelou, from
Wouldn't Take Nothing for
My Journey Now (As spoken
by Ms. Angelou's grand-
mother, Mrs. Annie Johnson
circa 1903)

Station 1
Hit the Pause Button

Station 1. Hit the Pause Button

One inescapable ingredient in the quest to become ourselves—like getting wet when you want to shower—is to slow down. This station invites you to allow in quiet spaces of "not doing." You begin to unplug more often from distractions and busyness. You pause to take inventory—to recognize that your current path and operating style may not be leading you to the life you're meant to enjoy. There are selected tools here to help you to stop, look and listen. Hitting the Pause Button can be a life phase (a period of slowing down and reflection) and something you can do literally several times a day. Each pause is a chance to reclaim your true spirit and adjust your steering.

Why Hit the Pause Button?

I don't need to convince you that the world keeps increasing speed to the point now that it feels as if some giant finger were pressing "fast forward" all the time. That's why I'm urging you to create soothing, restful spaces in your life. My greatest teacher in this art came in the form of a scrawny stray cat that wandered into our yard and ultimately into my heart. At a time when I needed to stop doing so much, he "forced" me to be still. I became a pupil of this furry Yoda on my lap. If we don't slow down and permit quiet to permeate us, we continue to miss out on the most beneficial inspiration and clarity we'll ever experience. Our go-go-go lifestyle is dangerous, for our physical, mental, emotional and spiritual health. And, contrary to popular work ethic fantasies, not taking time to pause can't be great for your long term financial health, either.

It's also illuminating to pay attention to the quality of your time-outs. Are you ingesting sugar or caffeine with an office gossip chaser, or truly refreshing your system? Hitting the Pause Button includes unplugging from all of the stimulus of cell phones, beepers, email, faxes, meetings, errands, soccer matches, dinner parties, TV, radio, and to-read piles. You want to disengage from outer distractions to begin to cultivate inner awareness.

You have already had a taste of Hit the Pause Button with two previous exercises, Take a Breath and Take a Hike. I challenge you to create more pause button times every week. Use a few conscious breaths to complete one thing before racing to the next. Breathe and choose who you want to *be* in a meeting. Hit the Pause Button fully when you greet your partner at the end of the day. Brew a cup of tea and savor a spot of quiet time. Linger in the shower. Listen to a CD without doing anything else. Let yourself stare out the window. You get the idea. While your inner critic may whine that these times are frivolous or irresponsible, rest assured that it is highly productive to shut down and restart your human system for more clarity, wellness and creativity. Here are two more exercises to equip you with worthwhile ways to Hit the Pause Button.

• • • • Take Five: Your Morning Ritual • • • •

One of the simplest and most beneficial life habits you can take on is a morning ritual. Do you wake up already thinking about your to-do list, while you gulp coffee and dash for the train? Is the morning more about perspiration than inspiration? Also consider the impact of digesting the morning news, filled with crime and conflict. How you begin your day sets the tone for the rest of the day. Each day adds up to your life. The purpose of this tool is to Hit the Pause Button for the sake of beginning each day consciously and intentionally. Just five minutes each morning can be the catalyst that makes the difference between tolerating your life and loving it.

There are 1,440 minutes in each day. Can you spare five to find more joy or effectiveness? Are you and your aspirations worth that? My morning ritual includes affirmations and surrender. (My end of day ritual is about gratitude.) Of all the tools I have created for myself and clients, these are my most enduring and treasured life habits.

I am not a morning person. Not yet fully awake and functioning, I shuffle into the kitchen. The dried cranberries I used to sprinkle on my cereal sit next to the salmon flavor cat treats in a remarkably similar package. You can guess the rest of that story. I share this personal tidbit for my non-morning comrades out there who might resist the idea of adding anything to their morning. At the same time, I must tell you how important a morning ritual is in our quest for Inspired Living. It doesn't need to be time-consuming or elaborate. Simple, short and sweet may be best, as long as it has meaning for you.

Morning is ideal for practicing your Tune In Time (introduced in Chapter 2). Imagine kicking off each day feeling guided by something greater than yourself, and supported to go for it for another day. Another simple morning ritual is reading something that inspires you for five minutes, such as *The Daily Word* or other daily meditation type books. Read affirmations or intentions that genuinely inspire you. (There are exercises later in the book to help you create these.) Try taking five minutes, three mornings per week, to start. Then build up to a daily habit. Over time, this tiny piece of your day will have a significant impact in how you experience and appreciate your whole life.

• • • • Take Inventory • • • •

Another important aspect of Hit the Pause Button is to assess where you are in your life. Here's a whole life inventory tool designed to reveal insights that don't come up in the daily grind, or even through typical goal setting. I have witnessed the seeds of transformation with this process, helping clients to gain clarity and set new intentions in motion.

To begin, don't start out digging for issues or problems to fix. For each area, first acknowledge what you *do* like or love. Start out with gratitude, acknowledging what you appreciate or feel blessed about. Look for the good and celebrate something, even if it's challenging to find positive energy. For example, in the category of "Physical Health/Body" my client Jackie celebrated that she felt in good health, overall, that she had found a wonderful acupuncturist, and that she was grateful for the healthcare benefits with her employer.

Now, move on to what you would love to experience in each category. I've been privileged to witness another fascinating evolution in my coaching work. If we start with "What do you want?" or even "What do you want to create?" that often leads to describing achievements and things to acquire. That's not bad, of course. However, if we start by asking, "How would you love to FEEL?" or "What is your desired feeling state?" it leads to the ultimate higher agenda. Let's continue with Jackie and the health category. In response to "What do you want?" she could say, "I want to eat right and exercise three times a week." Her *feeling state* answers included, "Energized, in integrity with myself, and a sense of momentum."

It's your turn. Take some time to complete the following chart (use your notebook for more writing room). Consider tackling one or two categories per day over a week's time. If you prefer to do this in one sitting, allow at least an hour for your thoughtful reflection. Be sure to let your answers come from your genuine heart's desires, not out of obligation or what your ego thinks you ought to feel or accomplish.

Whole Life Inventory/Desired Feeling State:

Category	"Celebrate"	Desired Feeling State	Insights, Comments
Physical Health/ Body			
Personal Growth/ Self Development			
Friends			
Family			
Partner Relationship			
Fun, Recreation			
Work			
Career, Longer Term Outlook			
Money/Finances			
Community			
"Making a Difference"			
Spiritual Growth			
Environment/ Home			
Other?			

Later in the book, we'll build on this to develop your vision and follow through to craft some concrete next steps. For now, just let this be an awareness exercise. This will naturally begin to influence some of your choices and behaviors.

People say that what
we're all seeking
is the meaning of life.
I think that what we're
really seeking
is the experience
of being alive. *Rudyard Kipling*

Station 2
Get Back in Your Body

Station 2. Get Back in Your Body

This station reinforces the benefits of using more than your head to create an inspired life.

The following tools invite you to try different body awareness, touch, and movement activities, uniquely suited to your own needs and preferences. All of this helps you to take advantage of this amazing resource that gets neglected when we live mostly from the neck up. You also gain strength and stamina for the adventure ahead.

Let's Get Physical

Hopefully, I have begun to convince you to see how your body (and mind-body-spirit integration) is an essential component of creating fulfillment and prosperity. This is not about improving your physical health alone. As mentioned, being in your body clears up channels to your inner wisdom and restores energy flow. Let's imagine that you came to me saying, "I want to focus on enhancing my career and leadership at work. I really want a stronger sense of my life purpose. I don't want to invest any energy in being in my body. That's not of interest." I'd want to honor your preferences, of course. I'd also be inclined to respond that this is almost like asking for wallpaper and then saying, "I don't need the paste, thanks." Beyond the physiological benefits, being in our bodies helps us tap into states of *being* that transcend the hobgoblins of our little minds and open doors to our true fortunes. One of my clients is now seeing how working on the alignment of her spine opens up more possibilities for being aligned with the work she's meant to enjoy. Another client realized that dance classes helped her to move through her life with more grace and enjoyment. What if your spiritual enlightenment, life vitality and true success rely on you shaking your bootie? And guess what? You just might have fun.

Awareness, Touch and Movement

There are three aspects to being in your body I'd like you to consider. The first is *body awareness* - being in touch with how your body is feeling, your natural energy cycles and body signals. Secondly, you'll want to explore sensual body *touch* experiences such as massage and other healing bodywork to stimulate energy circulation and promote overall health and well-being. This will also facilitate getting out of your head. The third area is *physical movement*. All three combine in synergistic ways to advance continued growth, and mental and emotional vitality. This is valid in quick hits as well as with a cumulative effect over time. Sixty seconds of breathing helps you to become more centered. Sixty days of yoga helps you to feel more alive and connected to your purpose. Consistent habits like these infuse your life with a calm clarity. Tai Chi at 8 a.m. contributes to your ability to be less triggered and more productive in the 4 pm business meeting.

You may have noticed by now that I have not mentioned calories or cellulite. None of this is about trying to look like a Hollywood starlet, although fitting into your jeans better might be a very nice side benefit.

Find your own unique approaches for being in your body. If everyone you know is into Pilates and you've tried it but would rather have your teeth drilled, go find something else that works for you, your lifestyle and your body's inclinations. Don't make this about forcing yourself into an obligatory regime that's "good for you," like a gulp of castor oil. The primary goal is reintegration of body, mind and spirit. Find ways to awaken your body, get your energy circulating and put a smile on your face. Here is a menu of possible exercises, one simple idea for each aspect of being in your body:

• • • • Body Awareness • • • •
What is Your Body Trying to Tell You?

Use your notebook to start recording potential signals from your *body wisdom*. Do you have certain aches or sensations from your body? When? Why? Where is the stress in your body?

Where do you feel excitement or serene contentment in your body? See if you can engage in a sort of "dialogue" with your body signals and begin to understand the potential messages.

Here's a personal example. The night before a business trip, I had a terrible gut ache. During a meeting the next day, my gut was churning. I have come to understand that my stomach is like a B.S. Beeper, trying to alert me. After the meeting, another woman was popping antacids and a third colleague had a terrible neck ache. It seems most people have a zone in their bodies that goes off as a warning signal. Prompted by my literal gut reaction, I placed my hands on my stomach and pondered, "What's wrong with this picture? Is someone lying? Am I lying to myself somehow? Is something out of integrity?" It turned out that beneath a sugarcoated surface, there were nefarious political agendas brewing. That project was clearly not in line with my values. My body knew this before my thinking head realized it. When my stomach grumbles, I still ask, "Did I eat something funny?" but I don't assume that's the only possible cause anymore.

Listening and *dialoguing* with your body can become a life-enriching skill. The mind-body integration questions will help you think through choices, from career moves to family boundaries. Wouldn't it be nice to find value in body signals (including some pain) rather than only be defeated or annoyed by them? Do you have a body signal alert system that might actually be helpful to you? Start to actively notice and then get curious, musing, "Hmm, what is my body trying to tell me?"

•••• Touch: Not Just for Pampering ••••

Touch is the first of our five senses to be activated as newborns and, as we grow old, the last of our senses to shut down. Touch and bodywork are essential elements of psychological health, including enhancing mental patterns. Research confirms that therapeutic massage speeds healing, improves our frame of mind, boosts self-esteem and performance, releases emotions, and reduces anxiety. Aside from all that, it just feels good! We also need to understand the value of massage (and other body-work) as part of our *proactive* health and success habits, not something we reserve as a special pampering treat or when we're almost running on empty. Bodywork needs to be as much a part of your life as brushing your teeth or taking vitamins.

When's the last time you had a full body massage? Peruse the following menu. Select the one form of bodywork that appeals most to you and book an appointment. Your mission, should you choose to accept it, is to find a right-fit bodywork modality and practitioner for you, and make this a consistent lifestyle habit.

- Therapeutic Massage (various approaches)
- Reflexology
- Acupuncture
- Energy Healing
- Salon treatments (facials, aromatherapy body wraps, pedicures, et al)

• • • • Movement: Shake Your Groove Thing • • • •

We have already extolled the wonders of walking as a way to stir up wisdom or shift your mood. You can walk for cardio health, to pray, or to prime the pump for innovation in your work. I can't imagine a more cost-effective, convenient and beneficial tool.

I have enjoyed feeling joyfully connected to my true spirit while doing something called Trance Dance (see Resources), or even dancing to disco in the living room. Try this: put on music that will make you want to sway your hips. Close your eyes and just let your body move, without concern for what it looks like. Let yourself get lost in the music. There is an energy within you that aligns with the vibration of the music, the beat of the drums. This is a very efficient way of getting out of your thinking head, allowing that spirit of aliveness to infuse the cells of your body. In WUI workshops, I encourage people to move to music. In the beginning some people are understandably resistant, and may even think it's silly or irrelevant. After several weeks, they *get it* and love the benefits of the mind-body-spirit integration experience.

So, find your own way of moving. Walking and dancing top my list. You may tap into similar benefits from biking, swimming, rock climbing, or kickboxing. Find the movement that awakens your true spirit, and keep it up in order to *stay awake.*

For anyone who may be limited regarding physical movement, please know that the underlying purpose is to access your body energy and get out of your thinking head. No dance kicks of athletic prowess are required. Explore your own ways of being in your body and allow energy to flow through you, using music, breathing, or whatever else feels fun and expansive to you.

• • • • Questions • • • •

• What is your sense of how *being in your body* contributes to your overall life satisfaction and success?

• When it comes to how well you honor and care for your body, what's your current score (0-10)?

• Tune in to your body and imagine it's telling you what it needs and what it would like to try. *What does your body tell you?* Consider the following questions:

• How well-fueled are you nutritionally?

• How well-fueled are you with consistent, quality sleep?

• How well connected are you to your gut wisdom?

• How well-fueled are you with physical movement/exercise?

- How well-fueled are you with physical touch/bodywork?

- What baby step could you take to make progress in one of these areas over the next few weeks?

The minute *you*
settle for
less than you deserve,
you get even less
than what you settled for.

Maureen Dowd

Station 3
Explore U

Station 3. Explore U

Think of this station as a sort of graduate school—having fun pursuing an advanced degree in *You*. Tools include ways to cultivate more self-observation, such as the Spy on Yourself game you've already seen. We collect clues to uncover core values and other key inspiration factors. Another aspect of this station is learning how to build habits for self nurturing and acknowledgement. Ultimately, this station equips you to cultivate the most important relationship you will ever have: with yourself and your true spirit.

Collect Clues About Your Passions

Go hunting for insights about what makes you tick… and what makes you hum, dance and fly. It's worth pointing out that we're *not* focusing on weaknesses or looking for things to improve. Rather we want to emphasize recognizing your natural strengths, tendencies and magnetic pulls. You've already started this process with the Values exercise from Chapter 3.

In Wake Up Inspired groups and private coaching, we have fun hunting for clues that reveal one's passions, gifts, fulfillment factors and purpose. Notice below that I use the word *play*. I invite you to have fun with this. Also, if you ever feel a bit stuck when trying to answer questions like, "What are your passions?" please know you are in good company. For most people, that's just too direct a question, and can lead to feeling frustrated rather than finding breakthroughs.

Here are two principles to keep in mind about uncovering your own passions: 1) Sneaking up on them with questions that come in through the back door is usually more effective. 2) Let your passions become clearer over time. Let's get you started with one of the favorite WUI games.

• • • • **Play With Hats** • • • •

Imagine a cosmic cat has granted you nine lives. She wants you to describe each of those lives, with a bit of flair, just having fun playing the game. None of this has to be super sensible or logical. Let your creative side come out to play without concern for being able to actually live the lives you invent. They can all be far-out fantasies, or you can include some more within reach. It's just a game. Imagine a table of hats that you might find in the costume room of a theatre. For each of your nine lives, grab a hat (or imagine any other kind of prop, if you like) to help establish this role. Then, tell your cosmic cat what you do in this life and why it's so great for you. There's no need to push out all nine lives at once. Start with a few in one sitting and add more over time, perhaps one a day, for a while. Ready? For each of nine lives, describe the following:

• Hat (or other prop)

• What are you doing? What are you up to in this life?

• Why is this a great life for you?

If you need a little inspiration, here are brief summaries of some of the lives that three of my clients came up with during this game.

Jade's Lives

1) Captain's hat, life preserver/ Sailing my own 60 foot sailboat, docking at my B&B in Western Australia/Great because I love the vibe of sailing, enjoying life and helping a variety of different people enjoy hospitality...

2) Camera, Tripod/ International photographer/ Great to travel all over the world and capture provocative portraits of people in everyday life/Enjoy being well known/ I love the different lifestyles and cultures, capturing essence of people (not a staged pose)...

3) Legal pad/Mediation attorney, arbitrator/Great to help small business owners resolve issues/ I enjoy being in that counseling role…

4) Ballet costume/Dancer, "Giselle," part of international troupe, ballet, flamenco, have a flat in England/ I love the creative expression and physical discipline…

Wow! If you shared this menu with a job placement person, he or she might say that this is too scattered to find a match for you. Good thing the purpose of this game is to collect clues about underlying passions and fulfillment factors. The core themes (from those clues) can later be applied to "real life" in more pragmatic ways. Across most of Jade's fantasy lives we find a fascination with people. On the surface, the sailing and B&B fantasy is all about freedom and fun. However, there's also that thread of relating to people of different cultures. It's similar to the mediation energy, being the bridge or harmonizing force. You get the sense that with Jade, people will feel genuinely seen and heard. Jade's passion will help them to relate better and enjoy life more. There's another theme about variety, with all of the international references. In listening to Jade, you could also detect that discipline was a strong theme in each life. At the same time, she needs enough of that "wind in your hair" vibe in her overall life to feel at her best. All of these data points inform Jade's clarity of knowing who she is. They help her to play with scenarios for consciously creating her life in the future. They also influence her day-to-day choices for now.

Debra's Lives

1) Big Southern Belle Hat/Married to a wealthy man/Great because I love being a woman who lunches and enjoys lots of leisure…

2) Shoes/Single woman like Sex in the City, "Zoe"/ Great because I love the hip New York lifestyle and everyone comes to me for recommendations on the best deals in designer clothes and consignment furniture, where to dine…

3) Cell Phone/Art Dealer/Great because I'm helping people with just-right taste in art and knowing artists...
4) Fedora/Being a forensic detective/Great because I love searching for clues and the science/Respected for my opinion and enjoy being top of my game, I show up at the scene, do my thing and leave, love the freedom of having no set schedule...

This game led to insights for Debra that highlighted a passion for "squirreling out" things, such as searching for great finds in a flea market and having an eye for design, color and what will work well together. There was a consistent theme of being independent, which helped Debra recognize that she sincerely did not like most aspects of managing other people in her job. She did have a passion for teaching and mentoring, however. That was an important distinction. This led to her discovering new ways to leverage her expertise, rather than completely abandoning her field and starting over. It would not serve Debra well to open her own business and feel the weight of being the boss for 20 people. But it could be very fulfilling for Debra start up a business concept in which she trains 20 people (or more) each year. You can also see clues about a certain amount of glamour and urban lifestyle in Debra's fantasy examples. These may be important life ingredients to keep in mind.

Cynthia's Lives

1) Map/Truck driver/Great to be exploring USA, at my own pace...
2) Wings/Being a bird/Great because of the perspective, freedom to move and change...
3) Different kind of wings/Being an Angel/Great because I love helping people, not worried about being the top dog...
4) (no prop)/Being a star (celestial, not Hollywood)/Great because it includes hopefulness, a sense of light, brilliant and disappearing...

I share Cynthia's examples for a couple reasons. First, she really let her imagination take flight, going so far as being a bird, an angel and a star! So, let this inspire you to freely play with whatever comes to you during this exercise. Second, it's fascinating to notice the huge chasm between the surface view of a truck driver versus a celestial star. However, all of these examples carry a theme of *flying free* in various ways. Cynthia would be wise to seek out experiences that allow her to feel free, unencumbered and maybe even to soar.

•••• It's Your Turn to Play ••••

Once you have generated at least nine lives and feel satisfied with playing this game fully, it's time to shop for insights. In reviewing your own imaginary lives, sniff out some of the underlying values, passions, or other clues that make sense to you. Don't take things too literally. We didn't conclude that Jade should open a B&B in Australia or that Debra should move to Tennessee looking for a sugar daddy. Look for your consistent themes, including noticing what is *not* included in your fantasy lives.

What insights can you glean for now that will help you to be more in sync with who you are meant to be?

Neither a lofty degree
of intelligence
  nor imagination
    nor both together
go to the making of genius.
  Love, love, love, that
is the soul of genius.

Wolfgang Amadeus Mozart

Feed a Passion: Mr. Smith Goes to Cooking School

Here's a story that underscores the importance of feeding your passions. Craig Smith came to me with a popular lament. "My job is making me miserable. I just need to find a new job and that's it." Craig was getting a bit crispy around the edges and craving some sort of a breakthrough. We met to launch his coaching, exploring his needs, goals and so on. I really liked Craig and my soul wanted to see him feeling more alive and fulfilled. I was listening for any seeds of passions or inklings of callings. Craig's responses were somewhat flat and not all that illuminating. He wasn't uncooperative, just a bit shut down by now.

A pre-meeting package included questions like "What would you do if you won the lottery?" and "What would you do if you discovered you had one year to live?" He had left these blank. As we were putting on our coats to leave, this voice from behind his collar said, "I know what I'd do if I won the lottery." I leaned in. Finally, we might have a nibble toward a potentially meaningful revelation. He continued, "I'd go to cooking school." My heart jumpstarted a bit.

To fast forward the story, Craig enrolled in a part-time culinary arts program. We also worked on being in touch with his core values and thinking patterns, and making conscious choices that could proactively create fulfillment. Now, here's the core point of this story. Craig came to coaching calls reporting, "Marian, the funniest things are happening…My job isn't so bad lately…I'm getting along with my wife even better…Communication with my daughter has opened up." Other positive shifts continued. Over several months time, Craig and I agreed that there was an intriguing synergy going on. It's fair to say that if his job felt toxic, that negative energy infected other areas of life, causing a general malaise. By feeding his passion about cooking school, Craig fostered a shift in positive energy that began infiltrating the rest of his life. This made the job change less pressing, if not irrelevant. What mattered most was his ability to know himself and create a rewarding, whole life.

There's also wisdom to glean about starting with your *heart* and not only trying to fix the one thing your head tells you to correct. Try not to put all of your fulfillment and identity eggs into one basket. We need to consciously spread our fulfillment across multiple areas. If we had only focused on surgically removing Craig's "bad job," we would have missed out on the breakthroughs that seemed to sneak in through side doors. Even if you know precisely which aspect of your life you want to zero in on, please keep in mind a whole life perspective. Each part of your life has a potential domino effect on everything else.

•••• What Feeds You? ••••

It's important for each of us to know what feeds us and then do our best not to deny those sources of fulfillment. Don't think only of big livelihood scenarios. Notice the smaller passions that may need to be in your life for you to flourish. It's fascinating to watch clients return to singing in the choir or training for a marathon, and see how this contributes to who they become. When you contemplate feeding your passion, your inner committee may scream, "I don't have time!" That may be true. Yet when we say "I don't have time," what we're often saying is: "I don't really choose to create the time."

Consider the potential benefits of making the time. What passion would you just love to feed?

•••• Questions ••••

• What would you do if you won the lottery?

• What would you do if you had one year to live?

Try to go for 20 or more "items" in answering the above two questions. Notice which responses feel truly worth your attention.

- What might be a passion that could be fed (beyond some of the fantasy answers to above questions)?

- Scan your memories for times when you felt fulfilled and energized. What once gave you joy and has now fallen off the schedule? How could you feed that passion again? What could start as a little experiment for now?

You have to find something
that you love enough
to be able to take risks,
jump over the hurdles
and break through the
brick walls that are always
going to be placed in front of you.
If you don't have that kind of feeling for
what it is you're doing,
you'll stop at the first hurdle.

George Lucas

Station 4
Make Room

Station 4. Make Room

Contrary to our cultural inclination to add stuff in order to feel better, the quality of our lives can be enriched by letting go of things and ideas. The primary intention here is to reduce blocks to your optimal energy flow. You'll want to start "clearing" and "completing" things that you have been putting up with, or putting off. The clearing may be literal, such as purging old clothes and kitchen gadgets from the attic. It may also include shedding self-defeating behaviors or beliefs. Completing things might include handling unfinished business or other distractions. Essentially, this station equips you to make room for the abundance that is meant to come into your life. Here are a few exercises that will lighten up your energy without much heavy lifting:

• • • • Play with Pruning Shears • • • •

In my husband's gardening books, they talk about "energy suckers" - those parts of a plant that must be pruned in order for the energy to be properly channeled to where you want it to go, such as into that big, juicy tomato. What are the "big tomatoes" in your life? What are the energy suckers that drain your time or capacity to devote effort to what you'd really like to be doing? In business, certain projects or clients can be like energy suckers, not allowing enough energy to be channeled toward that right-fit, profitable, super-rewarding work. We might rationalize about having a bird in hand and hang on to short-term cash flow. While we let these potential drainers linger, we neglect pruning and prohibit our true prosperity.

Imagine me handing you a magic pair of pruning shears. Imagine walking through the areas of your life, as if through a garden, pruning shears in hand. Using that metaphor of energy suckers, start to notice where you want the nourishment to be effectively channeled. What are potential distractions that could use some pruning? Pick just one small focus and commit to some way of pruning an energy sucker to make room for one of your juicy tomatoes.

• • • • Out of the Closet • • • •

Spend an hour in your clothes closet, and pull out anything that a) is a low-self esteem outfit (you know the ones), b) you have not worn in several months to a year, or c) you can't say for sure you will wear again. Consider scoring items 0-10 for how well they fuel your sense of true self or prosperity. Give away anything below a 6. It may be a "10" for someone else, so let that energy flow.

• • • • Break Free from Your Tethers • • • •

What are some of the old stories, beliefs or resentments that may be limiting your forward movement? I call these "tethers." As this label suggests, these can be chains to your past or perspectives that prevent you from going beyond a certain radius of possibility. Self-perception is a pivotal tether. For example, what do you secretly believe about your worth and potential? What are you not willing to forgive yourself for and move on?

Imagine yourself attached to invisible chains. Where do you feel "yanked back" or unable to progress further? Is there a subtle self punishment over something from your past, such as "I should have done such-and-such when I had the chance"? Is there lingering resentment toward a person or group? Get curious (and compassionate!) about your possible *tethers* and write about them in your notebook.

Now imagine really letting go of this old stuff and seal the deal with a releasing ritual. We scatter ashes at memorial services and make wishes while blowing out birthday candles because rituals help us to highlight what is significant to us. For your releasing ritual, write out your old tethers on paper and toss the list into a burning fireplace (safely, of course). Or release stones into a flowing river. You may want to declare something like, "I am now free of that old story about not being capable of creating great professional relationships." Have fun creating your own unique releasing rituals. I'm not saying that one toss into the flames makes all your limitations disappear. However, there is true power in rituals, because you infuse this with your thoughtful intentions.

My Left Tire

"I think there might be something wrong with my left tire," I said to my husband in that bizarre mode of *I'm just a girl and you're a boy, so you must instinctively know more about cars.* He valiantly went out to the garage, drove my car to the gas station and put air in the tires so his little woman would be safe. Naively, I thought it was handled. For several weeks I noticed that left tire looking low and would need to find a station and crouch down in the freezing, windy Chicago winter to fill it with air. I'm embarrassed to tell you how many times. In my crouching Marian pose, it did occur to me that I was not being a model of smart energy management, stopping for air over and over rather than getting to the root of the problem. I just kept putting it off, telling myself that I didn't have time.

There was a great life lesson in the metaphor of a slow energy leak, unattended at a deeper level, with repeated superficial attempts to treat the symptoms, not the cause. I also realized that I had to own this myself, not absurdly pretend it was going to just go away or pass the burden to my husband. One day the tire was almost flat, so I was virtually forced to handle it. Synchronicities led me to a very nice man who put in a plug. Again, I thought my left tire story was concluded. A few weeks later, the slow leak reappeared and the *crouching Marian, hidden problem* routine began again.

I finally created a proactive day of handling the tire and several other niggling issues that were adding up to a collective energy drain. A different tire shop man found a screw in the tire and patched it. When I asked how long this patch would last, he proudly replied, "Forever." "Until the next screw," I added with a smile. My secret life lesson of that moment was that even when we think we've handled something, it might reoccur.

This process of noticing energy leaks, repairing and making room for new abundance to come in is an ongoing habit. I named this day "FREE" for Finally Reclaiming Energy Errands. It felt great to check off half a dozen little drainers and feel like I had more energy available to channel toward my true priorities.

I share this story to prompt you to notice possible slow energy leaks in your life. Where are you losing air a tiny bit at a time, and attempting to put on a band-aid rather than handle the root cause? This could be literal or more symbolic. Are there unattended house repairs that are draining psychic energy every time you enter a room? Is there a professional situation that's loosing air bit by bit that needs attention? Do you sense something unsaid in a relationship? It's amazing how a modest collection of small things can become an inefficient or even harmful disturbance.

•••• Reclaim Your Energy ••••

Do you need to schedule a day (or take 15 minutes each day for a while) to patch up leaks and redirect your energy? You'll love the feeling of reclaiming the energy from those little leaks. For me, it was just a tire, and I felt lighter the whole week after taking care of it. How could you build this into your life habits?

One learns first of all
in beach living
the art of shedding; how little
one can get along with, not how much.

Anne Morrow Lindbergh

Station 5
Assess Your Investments

Station 5. Assess Your Investments

This station helps you gain confidence about how you invest your energy. In the WUI program, this includes getting a grip on how you invest your time and money. More importantly, the tools equip you to start assessing things in terms of your *life energy*. There are exercises to help you get smart about how well-fueled you are on multiple mind-body-spirit levels. We look at things like your ratio of giving and receiving. We explore what balance genuinely means to you and how to create that. There are tools to enhance awareness of how your actual day-to-day activities align with your values and authentic priorities. All of this adds up to you feeling more in command of your own energy. Here are three of the best tools to get you started.

Balance is Not a Math Problem

Over a glass of wine with a group of female leaders, one woman said, "I am so tired of all the talk about balance. Balance, schmalance! It's not real." I laughed and empathized with her annoyance. Balance has become an over-used buzzword, and we're all getting weary of this unsolved riddle. However, it's not a topic that can be swept under the rug. If we keep kidding ourselves about the value of more speed, more stuff, more working, and not pause to assess how we are really doing, we're just going to explode. Unfortunately, many of our attempts at balance are unrealistic, unfair and ineffective. Here's an insight I must share from the privilege of working with hundreds of clients, week by week: *Balance is not a math problem.*

We've all seen the advice in magazines that tell us to get our acts together in five easy steps and "do more in less time." This can lead to more guilt when it fails in real life. There was a phase in my frenzied work life when if one more person told me to "just work smarter" I was going to burst into tears or punch something. Well-intentioned time-management courses expect us to advance-plan and adhere to perfect pie charts with 35% of our time devoted to family priority A, 35% to work priority B, and

25% to personal priority C, leaving 4.998 percent for all the other unexpected inundations of life, and .002% to see a movie or have a cold. Yikes. Another myth: If we can just keep each of our plates spinning enough, without letting any of them crash, we'll have balance. I'm sorry, but that's not balance either. That's a circus act. Take a breath and repeat after me, "Balance is not a math problem. Real life doesn't work like precise percentages in a chart. Trying to live up to this standard is almost cruel punishment. There has to be another way." Now breathe again.

I have seen so many professional women finally exhale a sigh of relief and validation upon hearing this little spiel from me. What is another way? Our pal Einstein said you can't solve a problem at the level of the problem. We need to go above it, around it, or underneath it to achieve a breakthrough. I say let's abandon the math and focus on choice and fulfillment. As long as you recognize you are *at choice* and feel satisfied enough with your energy investments, this overrides percentages, hours and checkmarks in your to-do lists. This is unique to each person with widely different versions of what it looks like.

Let me offer some examples to illustrate:

Sally is opening a restaurant, a long-held dream in the making. She's putting in 16-hour days sometimes, and it might be this way for a few months. She's absolutely out of balance on paper. Yet Sally is wholeheartedly investing her energy in this crunch period because she's finally pursuing her juiciest heart's desire. She's in a state of love, not fear. She is choosing this nutty schedule consciously- for a while. Rather than fueling guilt for not living up to the math version of perfect balance, I'd encourage Sally to enjoy this ride. I'd also want her to be vigilantly alert to not push herself too hard for too long.

Winston has been on a busy executive track for 20 years. He's just resigned from a job and is exploring new livelihood possibilities in coaching. After some lively discussions about his passions, strengths and potential challenges, we both agreed that it felt right to "step away from the painting" and not overwork this process. His homework was to *not* do anything about career and wholly indulge in self nourishment and play for a couple weeks. For Winston's phase of life renewal, this feels like a wise investment of his time and energy. This is his flavor of balance for now.

Maria is a successful business owner and frequent traveler. From the outside looking in, many casual observers would think she works too much and needs to chill out. While I am certainly a fan of chilling out, it's dangerous to leap to assumptions about what's actually beneficial for Maria. We check how "pleased, proud, and grateful" she feels about how she's investing her energy. I also encourage her to be true to her own authentic priorities and sources of fulfillment, and to avoid defining balance by how her life looks to others. Would we have called Mozart a workaholic and told him to spend less time on music and to take a work-life balance seminar?

With these three slices of very different lives, how could any one measure of balance be right for everyone? Also consider the bigger picture over time. Balance is a constantly moving, fluid condition. Evaluate your life in large windows of time, rather than beating yourself up for not devoting 2.25 hours every single day to quality self-care and personal growth.

The poet of corporate America, David Whyte, offers us a powerful insight: the antidote to exhaustion is not rest. It is wholeheartedness. Let that sink in. True balance is not a win-lose competition of work vs. personal life. The word *integration* often works better for my life, since the borders of work and personal play are blurred. When I am attending a lecture or creating a new tool for the Wake Up Inspired program, am I working or playing? The answer is yes.

In the book *The Answer to How is Yes,* author and consultant Peter Block has noted that balance isn't about the tension between work and life. It is about what matters. Block states that spending more time at home will not necessarily resolve the tension between "what the culture has in mind for us and what is in our own hearts." Block continues, "Resolution lies in becoming more balanced between engaging in what has meaning for us and doing things that are useful and practical, or in a sense, instrumental. Being fully alive is to be in balance wherever we are."

Beware of twisting these arguments about choice, meaning and fulfillment into perverse rationalizations for working ourselves silly. The bottom line is to deepen your awareness, be courageously honest with yourself and cultivate the ability to become master of your own energy, choice by choice.

• • • • Check Your Balance • • • •

Grab your notebook to check in about what feels true for you.

- If the word "balance" didn't exist in our vocabulary, how would you describe what you really want? What does that tell you about how to assess your time and energy?

- Balance must be unique to each individual. What does balance mean for *you* (for now)?

The Ultimate Power Tool – "Read Your Meter"

We don't really manage time. We manage our energy and our choices. Rather than equip you to be proficient at typical time management techniques, I'd much rather support you to be a more conscious investor of your precious energy. The next tool is incredibly simple, and it could change your life if you actually use it well. Have you ever seen pictures of the applause-o-meters from TV game shows? Well, imagine one of those half circle gauges with a needle. At one end is "Gratitude." At the other end is "Resentment and Regret." Try *reading your meter* daily for a while. Hit the Pause Button and take a meter reading of how you feel about how you have invested your energy that day. Where's your needle? Is it closer to Gratitude or Regret? Where would you like that needle to be? (Naturally, you'll want to also apply a meter reading to longer periods of time for a broader perspective. Where is your needle for that month, year and so on?)

The next magic question is, "What could I do to shift that needle in the direction I want? What baby step, new choice, or tweak to my lifestyle could I make that would fuel more gratitude and pride in how I've invested my energy?" We established the concept of Awareness- Responsibility- Choice in Chapter 2. This Energy Meter is a perfect companion to that ARC, giving us a way to assess how much the choices we make are indeed in tune with our true spirit.

Energy Meter

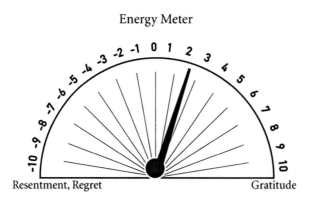

Resentment, Regret — Gratitude

We can add depth to each side of the meter. Here's a menu of possible energy check-in points for both sides of the meter:

Resentment, Regret	Gratitude
Disappointed, disillusioned	Pleased
Angst, disenchantment	Proud
Anxious, overwhelmed	At Peace
I wish I woulda, coulda…	On Path
Apathy	Passion
Restless	Purposeful
Panicky	Prosperous
Out of sync with my true spirit	Aligned, In sync
Confused	Called
Frustrated, Fried	Fulfilled

Scan both columns for possible meter reading check points. When you check in, do you feel more disappointed or pleased? Do you feel a sense of disenchantment or pride? You could notice how you are feeling relevant to what I call a "string of pearls"—Pleased, Proud, at Peace, on Path, Passionate, Purposeful and Prosperous. It would be overkill to assess all of these at once. Choose your most relevant points.

Create Your Custom-Designed Meter

What do you want to assess with a meter reading of your energy investment? What words best capture your most relevant and unique feelings? Boil it down to 1-3 key words for each side that really nail it for you and use those for your meter. If daily readings feel counterproductive, try 3 times a week or a weekly meter check in for a while.

There may be times when you're feeling "on path" in a work mission, yet restless about a relationship issue. Perhaps you'll want to apply your meter reading only to a certain focus area rather than a general check in. Use meter-reading insights as a way to increase your awareness and gently encourage yourself to make choices in the direction that feels right.

It's also worth making distinctions between genuine gratitude versus fleeting gratification. This is related to *finding joy* rather than enjoyment. When you read your meter, be sure to check in with your deeper energy.

By taking the time to do meter readings, Leticia was able to see that she was feeling more apathetic and restless (versus passionate and purposeful) when it came to attracting clients for her business. She had been working hard, trying to do all of the steps that would generate leads and so on. However, this energy meter helped her realize that her heart wasn't in it enough. We were able to refine her ideal client profile to renew passion and purpose. She could wake up more inspired and trust that this would lead to fulfilling work relationships and projects.

Which Comes First?

Earlier, I suggested that you ask yourself how you might tweak your life in order to feel more grateful. It's fascinating to notice the chicken or the egg phenomenon here. Does gratitude come from changing your life or does your life change because you are actively cultivating gratitude? The answer to both is yes. Developing a habit of appreciation is another substantial "tool" towards allowing your joyful life to unfold. A client once told me his definition of prosperity was, "Not having what I want, but wanting what I have." Research indicates that people who actively nurture gratitude are less anxious, more hopeful, and report higher levels of well-being.

• • • • The G-Force of Gratitude • • • •

Gratitude is a central ingredient in raising your vibration and attracting more rewarding experiences into your day-to-day living. Let your appreciation grow and watch a new spiral of positive energy help create the life you desire. Here is a menu of thought-starter ideas for cultivating gratitude:

Fall Asleep Counting Your Blessings

Imagine having an end of day ritual sealed with gratitude. Count your blessings instead of sheep, just like Bing Crosby advises Rosemary Clooney in the classic movie *White Christmas*. Try this: At the end of each day, write down (or say aloud) at least three things for which you feel grateful. This practice is a very grounding, powerful tool that naturally helps you gain perspective. I say my "gratitudes" aloud every night before sleep. I start by saying, "I'm grateful for…" and review the day from waking up all the way through being in bed in that present moment. It might include "I'm grateful for snuggling with the cats this morning. I'm grateful for coaching with Jill… I'm grateful for the call from Tom" (and so on). It's a wonderful way to acknowledge each day and nod off with a smile.

Gratitude Party

Invite friends and friends-to-be to gather for a gratitude potluck or morning coffee. Each person takes a turn speaking about anything for which he or she is grateful (from that day or week, month, year— whatever you choose). Talk about what purpose gratitude serves in your life. (Caution: As you might imagine, not everyone will be thrilled with this idea. Even at Thanksgiving dinner, my relatives roll their eyes if I suggest we each share a bit of gratitude, and so I just let it get laughed away. Choose your audience selectively for this one.)

Gratitude Letters

Reflect on your gratitude from this year. Who would you like to acknowledge with a special note? Who do you admire and appreciate? What organizations are you grateful for in your community? Let them know. Send a thank you card to your local firefighters and other unsung heroes. What other ideas come up for sending out gratitude letters?

Gratitude Grabbers

Carry small blank cards with you as a reminder to capture moments of gratitude.

You may want to give yourself a quota, such as filling a drawer or pocket with 3-6 gratitude thoughts each day. You could review your cards at the end of the week for a meaningful Pause Button experience.

He who binds himself to a joy
    Does the winged life destroy;
But he who kisses the joy as it flies
    Lives in eternity's sunrise.

William Blake

Station 6
Strengthen Your Spirit Connection

Station 6. Strengthen Your Spirit Connection

This station encourages you to have fun exploring various ways to connect with inspiration and guidance. There's an invitation here to expand on our typical spiritual ideas and practices. Go beyond notions of silent prayer in a holy place. Anything that makes you feel more connected to your own true spirit (or "closer to God" or "one with the universe") could be a worthwhile spiritual practice. Please don't let language or assumed rules get in the way of your feeling well-held in a flow of energy that wants you to thrive and prosper. Be open and experiment. Gyrate your hips, play with drumming, sing, have fun and let your inner artist get lost. Of course, you may also relish prayer in a place that feels sacred to you. This is about cultivating your intimacy with divine energy - however you feel moved to experience this. You've already been introduced to Tune In Time and dialoguing with your spiritual support team. Also consider the following tools to help you detach from the daily grind and enliven your spirit.

Get Lost

Get lost ... to find your true spirit. Let yourself get lost in activities that take you out of your plotting head and feed your innate creativity. This is often called a state of grace. I also think of it as feeding your inner artist or "soul food." You don't have to be an actual artist to have an inner artist that wants feeding. Recall when you have had moments like this - perhaps while gardening or rehabbing your home. What creative expression intrigues you, such as doing something with your hands, or taking an improv class? That's the inner artist in you.

Getting Lost stirs up another part of your brain and awakens energy that will contribute to longer term callings. It taps into *who you are meant to be.* This in turn fuels more alignment with your true spirit in other aspects of life. I recall being obsessed with painting terra cotta pots for a while, just after leaving my advertising career. Coming off a very structured, plan-ahead life,

I loved just letting the paint lead me, having no idea what color blends would emerge as the acrylics poured into various trays. Creating collages is still one of my favorite "getting lost" zones. Working with clients as they create collages (or collecting visual images) exposes values and heart's desires in a way that talking doesn't always reveal. Don't discount these examples as cutesy crafts or frivolous child's play. Getting Lost can be a valuable ingredient in your overall life success and prosperity- just as important as things like smart nutrition or financial steward-ship. One business owner client of mine recognized that work-ing in his woodshop on the weekends was vital to his profession-al success, and his ability to inspire his team from Monday through Friday.

If your life is in transition, creative projects that involve the transformation of something can be especially rewarding. Find an old lamp or thrift store chair and let your inner artist have fun converting the object into its next generation of expression. If brightening up your life feels right, create a splash of color where there has been none by planting petunias in a window box or painting a wall a bold new hue. If you are typically tight-ly scheduled, results-driven and orderly, consider getting messy. Finger paint, make mud pies with little kids, build sand castles and let them wash away – and appreciate the process. You don't have to match the activity to any sort of life theme. Just allow yourself to become absorbed and invite your true spirit out to play. That's all that matters.

Getting Lost Possibilities

What would your inner creative spirit love to do? How long has it been since you've enjoyed this phenomenon? Here are some thought starters:

Clay, pottery, tile making
Jewelry making
Painting, finger painting
Drawing, calligraphy

Quilting, needlework, knitting, crochet, embroidery
Woodworking, remodeling
Cooking, baking, pastry arts, cake decorating
Gardening, flower arranging, growing a bonsai
Playing a musical instrument, singing
Playing with Legos (why not?)

Getting Lost activities seem to fall into two categories: 1) "easy access" activities that occur daily like cooking or playing piano for a bit, and 2) more structured, plan-ahead activities such as classes and special projects. Sometimes, if you're open to it, that *getting lost* state of grace can sneak in even while you wash dishes or fold laundry.

•• Exercise: Get Started with Getting Lost ••

To start, commit to a date and time to "Get Lost" for two hours. Go fishing, stir risotto, refinish a chair — whatever lets you feel immersed and makes you forget to check the clock. Create space without concern for end results. Just play and get lost in the process. After your first Get Lost date, have fun trying out different activities. Give yourself permission to experiment. Discover more about what truly feeds your soul. And let Getting Lost develop as a regular life habit.

Poetry often
enters
through the
window of irrelevance.

M.C. Richards

Get Away

Many cultures throughout history have traditions of going off into the forest or desert as part of a deep transition and rebirthing process - as a way of moving into the next phase of life or role in the community. If you sincerely want to give yourself the gift of waking up inspired, it will benefit you greatly to create a retreat experience to connect with your true spirit.

Once upon a time, I ended up in the Maine woods, more or less by accident, for a trip that changed the course of my life. It was back in that era of working 60-80 hours per week and feeling hindered by my endometriosis. Being Miz Efficient Executive, I had booked a seminar on "How to get healthy in 7 days," and then some vacation time with my husband. I traveled thirteen hours to the middle of nowhere, only to discover the seminar had been cancelled. For the first time in more than 15 years I was "forced" to be schedule-free for two weeks in this breathtaking, tiny town where the mountains meet the sea. This was such a gift, providing a rich taste of "being" energy that invited my soul out to play.

It took a while to wind down, and then I just started walking. Walking became hiking. Hiking gave way to an unplanned vision quest. Many days were spent on the mountain, soaking up the nourishment of this indescribable energy. I melted into meandering, sketching, journaling, breathing and daydreaming. I met someone I hadn't really known before— this intriguing woman named Marian, with a big heart full of dreams, freckled knees and much love and light to share. I could actually see the difference in the mirror. There was an *aliveness* in my eyes. That time on the mountain was a profound step toward abundant health, rich relationships, true prosperity, and ultimately to this work and life I love.

I've joked around with clients that they need to be kidnapped and plopped into the woods for a week—with no workbook or fancy training. Obviously, your callings may lead you to very different settings. Where shall you go? Listen for your longings. I highly recommend that you make this a solo journey rather than travel with your partner or friends. If you must take the trip with others, create separate time for you to enjoy enough solitude and invite in the spirit connection you wish.

···· Exercise: Take a Soul Train ···· (Plane or Automobile)...

How would you love to custom-create your soul getaway retreat? Start a file to collect inspirations for your excursion. Tune In to keep your longings alive and actively seek information and ideas. Ask friends for suggestions about creating a spirit connection retreat. Try an internet search or check magazines for holistic spas and retreat centers. Pay attention to your intuition and notice areas of the world you feel *pulled* to visit. (Discern between earthly desires and spiritual nudges. I am magnetically *pulled* toward a furniture sale, but I know the difference between this and a deep craving to walk along the ocean in Santa Barbara.) Collect images and clippings that evoke your yearnings. Do you want nature and solitude? What will help you experience yourself as a human being more than a human doing? When your retreat vision has taken some shape, commit to dates on your calendar (what feels right: a weekend, a week, longer?). Block out this time as *not* preemptible. Book your transportation and lodging to help you seal the commitment. I encourage you to not over-plan or over-fill this trip with classes, books or sight-seeing. Less is more here. Allow yourself plenty of *being* time and white space. Remember this getaway is for the sake of deepening your spirit connection, not for being a tourist.

You don't need to spend a lot of money for your spirit connection retreat. Challenge yourself to be creative and resourceful in finding low-cost lodging or house-sitting. Why not trade services for the use of someone's cabin and so on? You could also create a retreat without leaving your hometown or your home. What's possible in sending the rest of your household away if you prefer to be at home for your retreat? Tell everyone you are not available, turn off the phone ringers and unplug the TV. Consider swapping homes with someone. Ask your inner guidance for ideas and be open to delightful possibilities. Enjoy the *journey* and be open to whatever may percolate along the way.

Don't ask yourself
what the world needs.
Ask yourself what makes
you come alive,
and do that, because
what the world needs
is people who have come alive.

Howard Thurman

Station 7

Connect with Your Right Tribe

Station 7. Connect with Your Right Tribe

Station 7 encourages you to seek out and nourish relationships with the people and communities that truly support your highest expression, shared growth and sense of being alive. Various exercises equip you to discover kindred spirits who are meant to be your collaborators, champions, midwives, mentors and playmates. You also want to allow for adjustments in the people you consciously choose to have in your life. Be willing to transform or let go of current relationships while cultivating new connections.

Check Your Vibes

For soulful community, support, stimulation and fun, it's essential to connect with other people with whom you resonate. When I say Right Tribe, I am not referring to your family of origin or ethnic background. This is about resonance at an energy level. We could say "chemistry," but it's more like a vibration. There are certain individuals we meet where the vibration feels strong almost from the first moment we make eye contact. Love at first sight is not just a romantic phenomenon. Haven't you felt something similar with friends or work colleagues? You feel more at ease, more connected, or even infused with personal and professional nourishment from being with this person or community.

When you are in a phase of evaluating priorities and making new choices, you may find that some of the relationships in your life no longer feel right. This can be a difficult adjustment. Give yourself permission to re-evaluate relationships and group associations relative to your values, purpose, vision and who you are becoming. I'm not suggesting that you only associate with people for what they can "do" for you! Nor am I encouraging you to become a social snob that must have only a certain caliber of people in your life. Rather, I encourage you to notice how you feel *energetically* around people and places. Toxic relationships are obvious, while other vibes may be more subtle. You might be tempted to gloss over these sensations. I encourage you to bravely and honestly notice when you feel alive and nourished, and when you feel flat or "not really connected" with certain people. Notice if you're hanging in there primarily out of guilt, history or inertia. Also, let yourself off the hook for relationships that didn't thrive in the past. It's possible to start fresh.

Beyond editing what's not working, I also invite you to enthusiastically explore new Right Tribe connections. Consider your own callings and what you'd love to create in your life moving forward. With whom might you create alliances for that mission? You might find Right Tribe around a common passion, such as being more environmentally conscious. By all means, do *not* feel like your resonance should be related to a noble cause. A fascination with quilting, science or hip-hop music might be the thread that brings you together with your Right Tribe for whatever is meant to unfold.

My client Susan noticed that she craved something different in social situations. While her social circle had not changed, she found that she was evolving in ways that made her impatient with conversations about TV shows or work gossip. She could attempt to transform these gatherings to feed her cravings for more meaningful stimulation, or she could start shopping around for new Right Tribe experiences. Ultimately, she did a bit of both.

Another client, Mario, a leader in his community, realized that he benefited from personally connecting with admired peers outside of that community. Since most people in Mario's life looked up to him, he appreciated how this level of Right Tribe challenged him in refreshing ways.

Rebecca gained insights about her disharmony with her work environment, ethics and pace. It wasn't easy, but she set new intentions about finding a sense of Right Tribe in her professional life. She was able to start fresh in a new position with a culture that was more in sync with her values.

The bottom line is to be true to your own energetic vibe, to know what fuels you, and to keep making connections that feel uplifting. This includes looking at how you give and how you receive. Set an intention to have relationships and communities that bring out the best in you, and where you bring out the best in others.

• • • • Questions • • • •

Reflect on the following thought starters in your notebook. Consider discussing with a supportive listener (or coach/group).

• Step back and check in about what you really want to create in your life. What kind of support, inspiration, or camaraderie would be great for you? Who would you love to connect with to help you fuel that?

• Begin to define Right Tribe for you. Try filling in these blanks: My Right Tribe needs are well fed when I have people with whom I feel_____and we_____.

• Give a score to your current satisfaction with "Right Tribe" in your life, 0-10 (0 = not at all satisfied, 10= extremely satisfied).

• What are types of Right Tribe for you? Consider professional, personal, spiritual, community and so on.

• What are relevant levels of Right Tribe for you? Do you crave being challenged by others who might mentor you? Would you love peers to have for social fun or professional collaboration at an equal level? Do you need someone to be a patient listener or sounding board? Do you need a helper?

• Consider Right Tribe affinities relevant to the mind-body-spirit fuel I keep advocating. (Hey, why not go for efficiency?) Explore relationships or communities for walking, yoga, going out dancing, healthy dining or whatever recharges your spirit for now.

- What's most important about Right Tribe for you?

- What may want to shift *in you* in order to allow for more optimal Right Tribe relationships?

When Right Tribe Transcends Being Alike

So far, I have encouraged you to find those right-fit people with whom you especially resonate. We can't leave this station without also saying that, at our core, we are all Right Tribe—each of us is made of the same vital life force. I know you've had the experience of seeing past differences and finding your common spiritual or human bond with another person. Continue to nudge yourself to expand that practice. When you feel separate or tempted to judge, breathe and get curious about what you might have in common. I sometimes play a little game, trying to find something to love beneath a surface I don't like. Strive for empathy, not sympathy. You might remember that deeper connection of essential energy. Try this and see what it does for *your* state of being. In Chapter 1 we touched on how waking up inspired was important for us individually, and for a sisterhood of conscious women. We have a critical opportunity to practice honoring the tribe of our sisters, while also respecting that we don't all need to make the same choices.

A Right Tribe Sisterhood: One Size Dream Does Not Fit All

Rather than slip into being close-minded about what does and does not qualify a woman as *successful*, it's especially important for awakening women to support each other. The new story of Inspired Living must include a fresh way of celebrating diversity- the diversity of what "success" means to each of us. Let me elaborate with a tale of two conferences.

I recently participated in a Women's Summit sponsored by the University of Chicago Women's Business Group. In a visioning breakout session about the future of women, several top female business executives lamented the trend of some women *opting out*, and bemoaned the fact that female college students at prestigious business schools were now declaring that they planned to be stay-at-home moms. They had some compelling reasons to be concerned. They feared a loss of influence if the next generation of women doesn't continue to make inroads in boardrooms and on election ballots. A loss of independence for the younger women's potential future was also cited. The mature professionals noted too many desperate divorcees among their friends, who were women with no marketable career skills or means of support. Our opportunity is to serve as tribal elders, helping younger women to make their own informed, thoughtful decisions, while always respecting their ultimate choices.

At the same conference, in another session for entrepreneurs, the speaker encouraged everyone to get venture capital funding in order to grow multi-million dollar enterprises with hundreds of employees. Many women in the room were not jumping on her bandwagon. Instead, they expressed an interest in creating a better quality of life, rather than building empires that required an aggressive strategy, decades of long hours and high-stakes pressure. Meaning and flexibility trumped money and stereotypical power for some women. Beyond any one limiting idea of the "successful professional woman" is a new territory where conscious choices lead to personal fulfillment, whether success means taking a company public or taking your kids to the park.

At another business women's conference, I had a stirring lunch conversation with a woman who had a home-based cosmetics business. She confided that she felt like some of the white collar women were looking down their noses at her makeup samples and home parties. I cringed, feeling guilty for my own trespasses along these lines over the years. Looking into her eyes, I saw both her pain and her pride. Her gray hair and laugh lines told me she'd been around the block. She had courageously pioneered being a business owner in a way that made sense to her and she deserved our utmost respect.

Whether our work is about lipstick or leadership consulting, we each are a valid part of the new story of success. We can find Right Tribe resonance in being *women*, making our way through triumphs and challenges. Each time we belittle another woman's choices, we're guilty of "success harassment," and making it more difficult for women (and men) to create their own unique dreams. Such harassment flips both ways, affecting women with corporate budgets as well as women who wield baby bottles. My friend Sharon, a single, career-focused woman, has great passion and pride in her work. At a social gathering, a full-time mother asked her to share "What's new?... but don't talk about work!" I'm guessing this mom wasn't even aware of how unfair and unkind this prejudicial remark could be.

Let's scan four of my clients. Jane is starting a multi-million dollar foundation to empower women in third world countries with education, micro loans and health care. Halle is exploring how she can work part time (thus decrease her income) in order to devote more energy to her home life and feeding her own spirit. Diane is in the early stages of starting her own business, and adopting a baby. For Rachel, her "baby" is a precedent-setting concept for new product development in her industry. Who is the most successful? They all are, of course, each in her own unique way. I'll bet you would love and admire each of them, as I do.

With increased solidarity and less judgment, we can create a world in which women celebrate being female, and the American Dream of success in the 21st century comes in more flavors than we can count.

•• Reflect and Recommit to Your Sisters ••

1) Reflect on how you may have subtly or overtly judged how others "measured up" to your view of success, and the ripple effect this could have.

2) Consider the Right Tribe support you would love to have to freely pursue your own dreams. Also consider how much you contribute support to a Right Tribe sisterhood of women. As the famous Gandhi quote says, we each need to *be* the change we seek in the world, not just hope for change to happen. What would you like to take a stand for? What are baby steps you could easily implement to empower other women? Discuss this with at least one Right Tribe pal and then champion each other to keep it up.

On the human
        chessboard,
all moves are
possible.

Miriam Schiff

Station 8
Dive Deeper, Reach Higher

Station 8. Dive Deeper, Reach Higher

In Station 8, you will discover the potent combination of exploring your "heaviest" and "lightest" energies. The chief intention is to help you reach for higher possibilities. We'll start by visiting the darker side of our shared human nature, acknowledging the inner critic that can block your greater good. We'll dive deep to shed light on insidious fears and old stories that may still influence you. We'll reach higher to find that uplifting, encouraging energy that's also within you. You'll gain efficient ways to tame your critic and engage your inner champion. Ultimately, you'll be able to choose new story possibilities over inhibiting doubts or other self-sabotage.

An imperative part of Inspired Living is to become more aware of what's actually driving you. You don't have to dive too deeply to find these influences within you. Notice what triggers you or tempts you to give up. What propels you forward toward more inspiring energy? Here's a selected exercise to help you check *who's driving* and then move forward, inspired by your higher truth.

Beauty and the Inner Beast

You've been exposed to various premises about having an inner critic or "beast" by now. That punitive voice is like a backseat driver, attempting to undermine you at every turn. You are much more complex than good/bad or light/shadow, but for the sake of efficiency, let's play with binary categories for now. Here are a few ways to capture this premise:

"Beast"	versus	"Beauty"
Inner Saboteur		Your True Spirit
Old Story		New Story
Coming from Fear or Lack		Coming from Love & Abundance
Inner Critic		Inner Champion

Both energies exist in all of us. Your chances of waking up inspired stem from how much you let critical inner drivers influence your steering and how you choose to respond. In a timeless Native American story, a young warrior struggles with competing forces, depicted by two dogs fighting. One dog represents fear, criticism and lack, and the other dog represents hope, love and abundant possibility. Troubled by the unrest of these dogs' constant fighting, the distraught warrior seeks the counsel of the wisest, oldest Chief. "Which dog will win?" pleads the boy. With lines from a thousand smiles framing his mouth, the Chief answers, "Whichever one you *feed* more." So, of course, you want to amplify "Beauty" while taming the "Beast." What follows is an exercise to help you put that into daily practice.

• Trump the Beast's Gripes with FAITH Cards •

Imagine your inner beast harping at you. Write in your notebook to capture what this critical, limiting energy says to you. This is for your eyes only. Be brave and honest. Examples might include gripes such as:

> Who do you think you are to…
> You're too old for…
> You're always too scattered…
> You're lazy and …
> You're going to end up broke and…

Once you have your gripe list written out, pause and let out an exhale. Remember this is not the truth. It's just one part of our inner drivers. Everyone has inner critic thoughts. I coach some pretty amazing, successful people, and let's just say that no one is immune from this human condition. Inspired people have found a way to diminish these limiting energies by focusing on what I call FAITH. I'm not talking about religion. FAITH stands for Full Aliveness In Truth and Hope. Your faith in yourself and in a loving universe that wants you to succeed is your grandest choice of all. Once upon a time I wrote a little song to use as part of my morning intentions that included the line, "I walk in faith, not fear. In love and light my choice is always clear." FAITH statements are antidotes to your beast's gripes. In a moment, we'll share a few examples. First, let's bring in someone to help you create these statements for your FAITH cards.

Find Your Inner Champion

Sometimes it's easier to imagine another loving character giving you encouragement. It's like a bypass operation from our over-thinking heads to our true spirit energy. Dive deep *and* reach higher to find your Inner Champion- that energy that believes in you fiercely, that assures you that you are capable of greatness beyond what your ego/personality can let in. It may be easier to hear the beastly inner critics at first, but I assure you this Champion energy is also within you.

Try this exercise for connecting with your Inner Champion:

Close your eyes and breathe. Relax your body, release tension, and focus on your breathing until you feel more peaceful and tuned in. Connect with that place in you that is full of possibility and truth, creativity and power. Breathe into that center. Imagine wandering into a forest or some other natural setting. At some point you realize you are no longer just wandering, but have been called to this place for an important purpose. You're not sure for what, but you know it is for your highest good. Imagine sensing another being coming nearer. You realize this being is indeed your Inner Champion. How does your Champion arrive and come into view (on a horse, in a chariot, sparkling on a leaf, in a swirl of fire or simply walking up to you)? This Champion loves you, knows all about you, and sees the best in you and all that's possible. Imagine how your Champion appears and take in this essence. This Champion may show up as a serene guide, a warrior, a spirit ally or whatever your imagination reveals. (A client and I got the giggles over her Champion showing up looking like Yul Brynner from *The King and I*.) Have fun with this! What message does your Champion have for you? Listen.

If it's easier to frame this as an imaginary character outside of yourself rather than a part of your inner world, that's fine, too. Go with what works for you. Dictionary definitions of "champion" include *a person who fights for or defends any person or cause, a warrior,* and *anything that takes first place in competition.* Wouldn't it be nice to let your Inner Champion help you reach higher and win (versus giving more power to the beastly inner critics)?

Fuel Your FAITH

Now, select some of the gripes, such as those zingers that get you in your Achilles' heel. Imagine your Inner Champion encouraging you to replace each gripe with a new truth, in the form of an "I am…" statement. "I am" creates a powerful affirmation. Remember that FAITH stands for Full Aliveness In Truth and Hope, so create statements that inspire you. A great time to use your FAITH cards is during your morning ritual, infusing the day with the "story" you want to create.

Examples:

Old Story Beast Gripe	**New Story FAITH Statement**
You're too indecisive and will never make progress.	I am able to access clarity and focused follow-through. I can tune in to my inner truth and *know* what to do.
They'll never agree to your proposal…	I am doing my best to prepare and go for the best possible win-win.
You'll go broke and not be able to fund the kid's college account.	My true source of prosperity lies within myself and my abilities. The truth is, I have always capably created enough income, succeeding when I commit my heart and mind fully.

| He's going to be defensive and my points won't ever be heard. | I am learning more and more how to best communicate with him. I am gaining insights about how to be assertive with grace. |
| You have a lazy mind and don't really add value. | I am fully engaged in my true passions and make a difference where it matters. |

Hold the Sugar

Let's clarify something about affirmations and emphasizing positive thoughts. There's no benefit in kidding ourselves with sweet affirmations that have no sticking power. Many of us have been taught to create *best case* affirmations of what we'd love to achieve, stated in the present tense. You might remember the Stuart Smalley character, from Saturday Night Live, finishing with "And gosh darn it, people like me." The joke was how far-fetched his candy-coated affirmations seemed.

In a great little book, *Law of Attraction*, author Michael Losier nails a very important distinction. He uses the example of an overweight person looking in the mirror, reading his affirmation, "I have a happy, slender body." It's a spiffy affirmation; however, it actually makes him feel worse each time he's reminded of how far removed this is from current reality. This defeats the purpose of affirmations altogether.

With my clients, we develop affirmations that have sticking power by avoiding too much "fake sugar" or anything that instills more doubt. We'll test it out, asking, how does that *feel?* Is it credible enough and genuinely inspiring, or is it more like "Yeah, and then monkeys will fly ..." You want to find something that's both uplifting and convincing, such as "I'm excited to be consciously making self-loving choices with my schedule today." Losier also recommends what he calls an Allowing Statement – an affirmative thought that helps reduce doubt and reminds us of plausibility. Example: "Millions of people have successfully lost weight and gained vitality."

One of my clients was resistant to things he viewed as feel-good fluff. He's a sweet person. He just hated language or exercises that felt too *sweet*. Thank goodness we could laugh together about this and hit on another important distinction. We clarified that we were not trying to turn him into a constantly cheery personality, living in unrealistic la-la land. We just wanted to find ways to put positive energy to constructive use. I've kept a little carved wood train in my office for decades, to remind me of the power of affirming thoughts. In the classic children's story, the train didn't keep saying, "I'll never make it" or "I'm so behind schedule." For my client, we could channel the productive use of that train's essence—"I think I can, I think I can…" without sacrificing his sense of grounded authenticity.

Don't Always Avoid the Dark

There are times when we actually need to move toward the fear or pain, rather than candy-coat it. With good intentions, we may notice a saboteur thought and respond with "Ooh, there's that nasty beast. Let's come up with an affirmation right away and focus on what I really want!" This can sometimes lead to what I call Premature Positivity. At times, it just doesn't make sense to "get over it." It feels like putting on a pretty, new pair of shoes and making a date to go out dancing, while pretending to not see or feel that 200–pound weight attached to your left ankle.

Now, of course you don't want to lament over the 200-pound weight for the rest of your life, moaning and pointing to your swollen ankle to anyone who'll look and listen. However, it's useful to get genuinely curious about when it's time to stop, turn and face your beasts. With clients, we'll play "Open Mike Night with Your Beast" and let that part have a rant. It's like shining light on something to more easily see how ridiculous it sounds, and also to help choose which inner drivers we want to "feed more." Then, it's smart to let that Inner Champion or a loving, encouraging energy to have the final say in the spotlight.

I was once invited to do a workshop with a group of prostitutes transitioning off the street and into smarter, healthier lives. We did this exercise with the beast gripe list and FAITH cards. We tossed the gripe list and kept the encouraging cards, suggesting that they use them daily for as long as this felt powerful. These women were remarkable examples of the triumph of beauty over beast, faith over fear. Most of us can't fathom what hardship and self-loathing they've been through. They found new hope, fueled by the voice of an Inner Champion. Their willingness to reach higher was so beautiful that they certainly won my admiration that night. If they can get over it, fuel new beliefs and take responsibility for new choices, I sure can. You can make the same self-loving choice, starting today.

• • • • Questions • • • •

What are you learning about the nature of your inner beasts? How much power might you give them by default rather than conscious intention? What are you discovering about your Inner Champion? Complete these in your notebook:

I am more aware of _____

_____

I promise myself (or my new intention is)

_____

_____

We define
ourselves by the
best that is in us,
not the worst
that had been done to us.

Edward Lewis

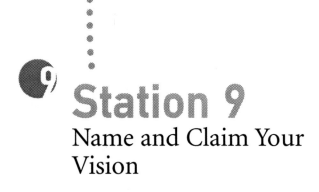

Station 9
Name and Claim Your Vision

Station 9. Name and Claim Your Vision

This station equips you to develop a compelling vision. First, you need to gain clarity in order to name your heart's desires. You will also need to claim your vision—to deeply breathe in a "Yes" that's both peaceful and exhilarating. You'll want to tell yourself: "I deserve this. I am ready, open and willing. I am happily taking responsibility for this intention. I am staking my claim. I am committed."

Let's get started. These next exercises will walk you through some significant and enjoyable ways to explore your vision.

Check Your Definition of Success

To name and claim your vision in a way that will sincerely inspire you, you must own how you define success. Let me share a story about that slippery word. I was once invited to a holiday party sponsored by a professional association. I clean up just fine and speak publicly without stage fright, but I'm also one of those people who inevitably dips a brand new silk blouse in the marinara sauce. It was one of those nights that I didn't want to have spinach in my teeth, a run in my pantyhose, or any other dents in the respectable first impression I wanted to make.

The elegantly chic president of this organization introduced me to a senior executive, saying that we had each recently been speakers at association events. He asked, "What did you speak about?" I had every intention of telling him my topic was "How to create the success you really want." What came out of my mouth was, "How to create the *sex* you really want." His eyes widened. While stifling a snort of wine through his nose, he politely continued, "Oh really, I wish I had been there. Tell me more!" (I must have redeemed myself somehow during the rest of our course-corrected chat, because he actually referred a coaching client to me.)

I share this story to help us remember that "success" can be a treacherous word. How that word may impact your vision requires care and reflection. Ask yourself: how have you been defining success? Who or what has been influencing that definition? Is your current definition really *yours*?

I remember that junior high school era, when wanting to be accepted by the cool group was equivalent to breathing at times. I was more than willing to shun my true self to be included— from the socially-shallow choices (shoes) to the potentially dangerous ones (smoking). How about you? Of course, we have all matured and gained perspective since then. Yet what has replaced the cool group allure in our adult lives? What insidious ways do we still crave measuring up and hanging out at the right lockers? How might we put ourselves at risk?

•• Reclaim the Success Meant for You ••

Write in your notebook as you explore your private, personal definition of the word *success*. Begin to fully acknowledge what you have inherited from cultural norms, peer pressure, and media conditioning. As you dismantle these assumptions, your own authentic interpretation of success will then have room to emerge.

Please take in the following questions more earnestly than you ever have before. Don't answer quickly. Take long walks to get out of your head and reflect. Spy on yourself in your day-to-day living. Commit to letting the seeds of these questions germinate for 30 days. Feel free to reshape the questions as you wish to get to the heart of what you want to clarify.

How is your definition of success influenced by:
- Your parents and family
- Your partner
- Friends
- Your variation of keeping up with the Joneses
- What you absorb in magazines, movies, TV, etc.
- The culture of your workplace/field
- Your neighborhood/community

Imagine taking all of those outside influences and inherited assumptions and setting them aside on a shelf, far away. Now, look within yourself. (I'm not saying that all of these influences are invalid. Nonetheless, you want to discern what is genuinely heartfelt and *your* true choice.)

Start fresh with a bare canvas and only your own true colors and textures. Try this: buy a blank canvas (or a large white flipchart sheet) and look at it every day for awhile, letting it call to you for your answers to "How do I define success?" Notice what resonates and sticks over time. If you like, jot down thoughts, draw, paint, or add images —-whatever helps you discover your own insights.

What is your own, unique definition of success? What is the deeper and higher answer for you and only you?

The hero's will
is not that of his ancestors
nor his society,
but his own.
This will to
be oneself is
heroism.

Ortega y Gassett

Connect With Feelings to Fuel Vision

Now that you're more grounded in the framing of your own picture of success, let's begin to sharpen your vision. If you're still feeling a bit hazy about what success wholeheartedly means to you, don't sweat it. The following tools will help you clarify authentic priorities and inspire your conscious choices as you move forward.

Often, a vision gets expressed in terms of outcomes - what you *wish to have* as an end result. I've learned to encourage my clients to first connect with *feeling states*. This is a much richer place to start the vision process. Let's look at a simple example.

Jessica is a busy professional who expressed a wish to have her house in order, including clearing clutter and unpacking boxes. When we probed further for what mattered most, we discovered that she truly yearned to feel a sense of peace and grace. As we thought things through, including how to juggle her home life with her leadership role at work, it became clear that expecting the house to be perfectly in order by X date would be a cruel entrapment, only adding to her high level of stress. Jessica's intention became "to create peace, move through life gracefully, and have the important things tended to." This was her way of naming her heart's desire. Jessica also learned to ask herself, "Am I truly creating peace and grace, or am I feeding the to-do list monster and kidding myself that *then* I'll have peace?"

From Wishes to Intentions

It's also helpful to make distinctions between a wish, a goal, a heart's desire, and an intention. Wishes can be well, wishy-washy. Your goals may be remarkable. However, they might also be like "shoulds" or the next logical move. Goals are often driven by something other than your inner spirit. A genuine heart's desire taps into inspiration.

Try filling in these blanks: "I would LOVE to_____" or

"My real heart's desire is _____." Feel the difference in that energy. Lastly, an intention takes your heart's desire one step further. It's a declaration of what you intend to create, attract or allow. The first step toward creating your true intentions is to clarify your heart's desires.

•••• How do you want to feel? ••••

In Station 1, "Hit the Pause Button," we asked you to identify your desired *feeling state* for various life categories. Let's build on that to develop your vision and primary intentions. Imagine it's about 12 months out (or whatever time frame feels right for connecting with your vision). Respond to the key starter question: "What do I most want to fuel, experience or create?" Your answer can be the same feeling state you previously put down (from the Station 1 exercise). Reflect for a moment to see if you want to declare anything a bit differently.

Here are few examples from a client, Helen:

Life Area:	Most Want to Fuel/ Feeling State:
Physical Health	"Energized, pep in my step each day"
Finances/Money	"Prosperous, delighted with the abundance in my life"
Work/Career	"Stepping up in my leadership, in integrity with who I am capable of being"
Community	"Plugged in"

Once you feel clear enough about your own desired feeling states, ask for a picture of what your life would look like if those feeling states were flourishing. What would it take? What is that vision?

Notice that I said, "ask for" rather than create. Yes, you are creating this vision. However, I invite you to *receive* it rather than force it out of your intellect. Let's bring in that Inner Champion character you met in the last station to help you with this. Remember this Champion loves you and sees you at your best. Close your eyes and ask your Inner Champion to show you a movie of what your life looks like with your desired feeling states present. Enjoy seeing various scenes of key areas of your life.

Flowing from her desired feeling states, Helen saw herself being more "plugged in" to community through volunteer literacy tutoring. She also saw scenes where she spoke her truth more at work.

A great way to develop your vision is to try this *receiving* process daily over seven days. Let your mental movie screen fill with the sights and sounds of what is meant to be for you. Try combining the following life categories over a week's period for your daily movie show times:

1. Health & Wellness, Personal Growth
2. Work/Career/Livelihood
3. Money/Finances
4. Primary Partner Relationship/Home life and Environment
5. Other Relationships; Friends, Family
6. Fun, play
7. Community Connections and Contribution

Each day, allow yourself to dream about your vision, letting the movie play in your mind. Consider a walk or a long shower to warm up your state of receptivity. Capture the most important scenes and sensations in your notebook.

At the end of seven days, you'll have a considerable vision to guide your choices. Of course, after letting that delicious menu of possibilities settle in a bit, avoid biting off more than you can chew. It's wiser to hone in on select areas, where you'll focus your attention for specific periods of time.

• • • • Select Your Top Intentions • • • •

Since it's counterproductive to tackle your entire vision all at once, try to narrow it down to three top intentions. That question, "What do you *most* want to fuel moving forward?" now applies to the most important aspects of your vision. These three intentions will be your top priorities over a 3-month period (or whatever time frame feels best for you).

Frame your intentions in a way that will feel uplifting and worth working toward. An inspiring intention generates natural enthusiasm and commitment. Inspiring intentions are what we do for the sake of love or passion—- our heart's desires set to the music of determination.

For instance, sense the difference between "reaching out to make a difference in people's lives and feel delighted with the abundance in my life" versus "increase income 30% by June." Go ahead and incorporate numbers and measurable accomplishments. Just be sure you're connected with real heart's desires. You want to feel inspired to stay in action.

Here's an example of three top intentions I created, including the feeling states:

1) Continue to fuel optimal health - feel consistently energized, enjoying vitality.
2) Birth next level of the WUI program - feel joyfully and productively in momentum.
3) Attract right-fit help and resources to fully honor this mission - feel lucky and amazingly well-supported.

Don't push yourself too hard by super-sizing your intentions. Depending on what's cooking in your life, your best initial focus could be in the category of self-nourishment. A smart intention could be something like, "To feel well-fueled. Emphasize filling my own well more."

These intentions will serve as your true priorities, your "Big Rocks" rather than the sand and gravel that can get in the way. You can include them in your morning ritual and incorporate them in daily or weekly follow-through. Sometimes we catch ourselves in pseudo-productivity: busily working, and clearly not lounging in a hammock; however, still not really progressing on the most important priorities. Use your top intentions as guides for how to consciously invest your energy. Set up accountability support with others to help you honor these promises you've made to yourself.

Consider using the following chart (in your notebook) to flesh out how you see your vision in action.

Vision Focus Area/ Top Intentions	What will it take to fuel that?	Next Steps?	Accountability Support?

Take a moment to consider the *claiming* aspect of this vision process. Assess how much you're ready, willing and open to say a big "Yes" to this vision. How much does this vision merit your respect and effort? How well can you embrace that you deserve your heart's desires? What would help you to fully accept, almost *expect* this vision to manifest in your life? How committed are you? Breathe, and then make adjustments to your vision or intention statements as needed.

The last component of the vision process, paradoxically, is to let go. Once upon a time, I went from having a burning vision to burning my vision - literally. I took the paper that featured my "Vision" and "Top Intentions" and set it aflame. This ritualized my declaration to leave myself open to whatever was meant to be for the highest good. The punch line of that story is that a wave of wonderful new clients flowed in, like this astonishing goodie bag of answered prayer. Being committed, yet not staying *attached* to a specific outcome, or exactly how things will unfold, is a key part of charting your course - which leads us to the next station.

Living your vision
is where
who you are
live. meets how you

Alan Amberg

Station 10
Chart Your Course,
Enjoy the Ride

Station 10. Chart Your Course, Enjoy the Ride

Once you've gained clarity on your vision and how you uniquely define success, how do you effectively create that in real life? In this station we explore structures for your ongoing navigation—how you steer through your planning and choices. This is where that blend of the mystical and the pragmatic especially comes into play. You want to be grounded in your values, purpose and vision. You also want to flow with inspiration and opportunities as they pop up. You want to find equilibrium between surrendering and "taking a stand." You want to create your own optimal blend of "allowing" and proactive, constructive actions.

Being a Good Steward

Previously, I asserted that Inspired Living does not flourish by just "executing the plan." You do, however, want to have some way of intentionally, consciously charting your course. You want to be a good steward of the inspired life meant for you. If I may be your coach in this moment, let me say that I'm not attached to how you plan. I do care deeply about how much you are letting your life circumstances, other people, inner critics and whatever else run you. Ask yourself how much the tail may be wagging the dog. I want to equip you to be the master of your own energy.

Let's start with a pivotal secret to charting your course effectively. The key is to *do it*. Doesn't that sound ridiculously un-clever? Nonetheless, I have observed that this is where things often fall apart for many bright, well-intentioned people. Understandably, life gets busy and people just don't take the time to develop or stick with a consistent "charting your course" habit. So, it seems wise to develop something simple enough that works *for you,* and then have the self-loving vigilance to keep it up. That's part of what people find useful in their coaching sessions. They're encouraged to check in about what matters most, to gain clarity about intentions, and to carry on feeling more focused and inspired. That's what the following tools will help you do as well.

The Check-In Versus the Checklist

We've all been through traditional approaches to planning and having a checklist to mark when we've accomplished each item. Consider also having a meaningful Check-In. Unlike a checklist, a Check-In is tuned in to your inner compass. It helps you notice how well you are steering as well as what new directions might beckon you. A checklist facilitates questions like, "Is it done yet?" and "When and how will it get done?" Your Check-In invokes questions like, "How am I doing with honoring my values and purpose?" Serving as a quick reference for your charter and mind-body-spirit fuel, it helps you to be more aware and to make inspired choices. Check-In questions lean toward "How is this feeling? What's working well? What's not? What am I learning about how to set myself up to flourish?"

I'm not suggesting that you drive yourself crazy with all of these questions every day. Personally, I like to focus on one daily question for a while. Consider creating one provocative question and then check in each day for a week (or weekly, if you prefer). One of my favorites combined, "What do I want to drive me? What do I *not* want to drive me?" This was a much more intriguing way to enhance my ability to wake up inspired than if I only asked something like, "Are my projects done when I said they'd be done?"

Your Compelling Charter, Revisited

For many clients, a key feature of their Check-In is their compelling charter (introduced in Chapter 3). The key ingredients of your charter are values, purpose and vision. As mentioned earlier, you don't want to let these navigation aids end up as pith on paper, but to actually apply them. Let's bring those pieces together to create your own charter now. The great news is that you've probably already done previous exercises designed to give you the components of your charter. Coming up, you'll see an example of my own Check-In summary page, featuring a snapshot of my values, purpose and vision. (If you like, peek ahead at this example, and then come back to build your own charter.) Check your notebook or revisit the following exercises:

Values

A values discovery exercise was offered in Chapter 2: "Spy on Yourself to Detect Values." Take that list of values and select the six that you most wish to focus on for a while. Which values would you like to have more of your attention? Choose values that are a positive motivating force, not just areas you think need improvement. Which values inspire you most for now? If you read them with your morning coffee, what would help set an uplifting intention for the day? This is the first component of your charter snapshot.

Purpose

Review "Peek at Purpose" from Chapter 2. What still feels true and inspiring? What other insights have you possibly come to understand about yourself since doing that exercise? Do you want to revisit any of the three trips to gain a sense of your core purpose? (You may also find clues about purpose in the "Play with Hats" exercise from Chapter 3.) For this charter snapshot, try to capture your purpose in a phrase. In my Check-In example, I used my core purpose statement: *I am the honking horn that won't let you be asleep to your true spirit.* I added a current mission statement: *I am on a mission to equip more people to wake up inspired and ultimately mobilize the joyful missions they are meant to live.* This is more specific to what I'm up to, as it applies to my day-to-day work. Whatever you create, let it inspire how you choose to invest your energy each day.

Vision

You worked on developing your vision and top intentions in Station 9. In my charter snapshot example, the vision highlights are a blend of intentions such as "Wake Up tour and book thriving" with the energy of FAITH statements. As an example, an inner critic may whine at me with something like, "Who are you to be the author and teacher about how to find inspiration and joy?" So, the antidote comes as "I am *destined* to speak, write, coach and teach…" If I fill my thoughts with these affirmations of callings each morning, I am moved to be a good steward of this joyful mission. It's a sweet, grateful vibe, not a boldly arrogant declaration. I can let go of outcomes (such as how many people come to a talk or buy a book) more easily, because I'm going with the flow of letting Spirit express through me, to the best of my ability. For your Check-In, let your vision and intentions boost your confidence about consciously creating your days in ways that work well for you.

OK, now let's look at the example of a Check-In.

Check-In

Compelling Charter Snapshot:

Key Values:	Always Spirit Led, "FAITH" & Abundance, Breathing Room, Aligned Action, Efficiency, Joy
Core Purpose:	I am the honking horn that will not let you be asleep to your true spirit.
Current Mission:	I am on a mission to equip more people to wake up inspired and ultimately mobilize the *joyful missions* they are meant to live.

WUI Vision Highlights:

I am a contributing voice in a spirited movement, stirring up "waking up" and inspiring others to reach higher, fill up their hearts and share their gifts in the world. I am meant to be a channel. I am destined to speak, write, coach and teach, letting Spirit express through me.

The book and Wake Up Tour are thriving. I love coaching with clients I admire and adore (X clients on X days). I am thrilled with the new website and other WUI offerings. I am jazzed about leading groups and meeting new people as opportunities for spreading this work flow.

Because of the WUI program, each reader/participant is feeling more connected to his or her own sense of true spirit. Ultimately, they become sparks of inspiration, contributing more conscious energy to their workplaces, communities, families and such. Collectively, we are vibrantly creating the new story, revolutionizing the way we create "success." I am living the new story today.

3-month Top Intentions:

1. Continue to fuel optimal health- feeling consistently energized, enjoying vitality
2. Birth next level of the WUI program- feeling joyfully and productively in momentum
3. Attract right-fit help and resources to fully honor this mission- feeling lucky and well-supported

Mind-Body-Spirit Fuel (ongoing, check-in list):

✓ Morning ritual & end of day ritual - Gratitude

✓ Tune in Time/ Angel Team / Sunday spiritual community

✓ Walking

✓ Water (drinking plenty and being around lake/ocean)

✓ Nutrition ongoing- morning protein shake, vitamins, grocery shopping, food program

✓ Weekly session with occupational therapist, Pilates stretches, massage

✓ Daily stretching exercises

✓ Self-acknowledgement, celebrating monthly.
Inner Champion chime-in

✓ Making Room- purging house, donations, etc. Breathing room, open vibe for new abundance

✓ Feeding the Inner Artist- singing, movies, dancing, home decorating, *playing hooky*

✓ Right Tribe people connections- Professional outreach, Monthly Dine Out group

✓ Hair & nails, skincare, clothing upkeep and refresh

************** Daily Check In Question **************
"How am I honoring calling over comfort?"

You can see that mind-body-spirit fuel is also part of this Check-In example, including habits like walking and drinking enough water. It all contributes to how inspired I feel and how productive I am while attempting to carry out my intentions. This Check-In example does not represent my entire life. My morning ritual includes intentions for my personal relationships with family, husband and friends. For my business, I might create additional planning tools with more specific tactics (such as the marketing plan described in Chapter 2 as an example of blending linear and metaphysical ingredients).

Creating Your Own Check-In

Remember— this is *your* Check-In, so it doesn't need to resemble mine or have the same ingredients. I just want to show you what is possible when you put these tools to work in real life. Together with my clients, we take time to build their charter and Check-In at their own pace and in their own unique ways.

With my client Sarah, we went through various exercises, including values-purpose-vision work. She also created a simple two-column sheet that captures the essence of her Check-In points in a different way. Here is one of Sarah's Check-In tools that I just love:

Old Me / Old Story	New Me/ New Story
Survive	Thrive
Other People's Rules & Expectations	My Mission & My Inner Compass
Inner Beast (letting it undermine me)	Inner Champion!!!
Victim	Hero
What Others Think = How I Feel	What I Feel, Think, Experience = ME
Authentic But Stifled	Authentically Assertive
Stuck [in this job]	Adventuresome
Planning for Someday	Experiencing Joy Now

Can you see how Sarah could use this to inspire her choices? This served as a powerful supplement to her specific intentions, as well as her ongoing calendar planning and to-do list.

Provocative Questions

The simplest Check-In could come in the form of one provocative question (such as the daily question at the bottom of my example). These are not meant to be answered quickly, and perhaps never answered completely. The idea is to live with the question fully. Here is a "Baker's dozen" menu of Check-In questions to stir up your own possibilities:

1. What is my soul whispering to me?
2. What am I digesting?... How am I nourishing my body, spirit and mind?
3. Who am I becoming?
4. What am I tolerating or putting off?
5. What am I doing to make room for new good?
6. How well do I respect my own time?
7. What would it take to really allow in the support I need?
8. What are my comfort zones? What does this cost?
9. What is present when I am contributing at my best?
10. What am I possibly resisting/avoiding?
11. What is inside of me that wants to be expressed?
12. Where do I find joy?
13. To what am I committed?

You can add the word "today" to the end of each of these to infuse your day with more intention and inspiration.

Planning and Choices Come Alive

As you may recall, the fourth element of your charter is "Planning and Choices." This is not another item to write down on your Check-In. It's an ongoing dynamic flow, which brings us full circle back to awareness-responsibility-choice. Too often, we are seduced into thinking we are already planning because our calendars are filled with meetings and to-do items. This is not necessarily conscious planning. It might just be order-taking. Stop and truly assess. Ask yourself, "Am I deliberately and enthusiastically charting my own course in tune with my true spirit and enjoying the ride?" If your answer is not "Absolutely," then you have room to tweak how you plan and practice inspired living. All of the tools in this book were created to help you feel closer to celebrating that intentional life. (The Energy Meter from Station 5 is a simple, yet effective barometer to keep in mind.)

I don't think you can follow anyone else's system to the letter and authentically manage your inspired life. In my first corporate job, my boss wanted me to use his project management system. His intentions were laudable, but I just hated this thing with color-coded cards and categories to track. That experience was a great learning laboratory for the importance of developing one's own methods for success. Please experiment with the concepts presented here and create your own made-to-order tools and habits.

Consider the following points to enhance your effective use of planning.

- Consistent contact— Ideally, how often will you refer to your Check-In or other planning tools?
- Accountability—How will you be accountable to keeping your promises, honoring authentic priorities, etc.?
- Portability – What is the best way to keep your planning system with you and allow for the ongoing adjustments?
- Adjustment—How will you build in flexibility, assessing what truly matters and what actually works? (This is a daily application of flowing with Awareness-Responsibility-Choice with fluidity.)

Let's clarify a sensible distinction about flexibility. All along, I've been encouraging you to stay fluid and accept divine order. However, there are times when we might too quickly declare that something *just wasn't meant to be.* There's a difference between knowing this intuitively and using it as a convenient rationale. Challenge yourself to sense and appreciate this distinction. When Plan A doesn't work out, don't immediately throw it in the failure or fate basket. Tune in to your inner truth. Let your higher guidance genuinely inspire you to try Plan B (C, or D…) or to let it go.

You may have heard the phrase, "If you don't take a stand for something, you're likely to fall for anything." My wish is that your planning structures will help you take a stand for what you believe in and want to express with your life—rather than letting *shoulds* run you or inertia creep in. Also try to recognize where you fall on the spontaneity vs. well-ordered, proactive planning spectrum. If you're a super-organized, rigid planner with every item check-marked from dawn until bedtime, you need to experiment with less structure and more open space. If you barely plan ahead, it's time to nudge yourself to experiment with more structure. By stretching beyond your normal routine, you will find ways to renew feeling inspired and getting into creative action.

Ooh, That Will Leave a Mark

A kiss from a beloved leaves a lasting impression. Bumping into a desk corner with your thigh creates another kind of imprint. You are always leaving a mark, whether you intend to consciously or are just bumping along. A word for leaving a mark is legacy. An inspired awareness of legacy is part of charting your course. (And can be literally included in your charter and Check-In tools.) We may associate legacy with grandiose ideals or the biggie projects we pursue. However, it's the tiny moments that also add up. With every conversation, meeting, facial expression and body gesture, you are having an impact on others. As you recall from Awareness-Responsibility-Choice, we accept responsibility for creating our own well-being and success. As we evolve, we experience another level of "good neighbor" responsibility for the health and happiness of our fellow human beings and the environment we all share. This is not a burdensome obligation. It is a joy-motivated choice. We naturally want to promote abundance beyond our comfortable, "got mine" zone of self-interest. To paraphrase activist and author Frances Moore Lappe, we slowly realize that we don't find hope. We become hope. Whining about "Why don't they do something?" gives way to "What am I doing to make things better?" (The context could be the global village, your family or your department at work.) This is one of the ultimate choices—to decide to be a person who contributes positive energy into a greater collective "energy field" of thoughts and behaviors. Consider what's called the butterfly effect from the meteorology domain: when a butterfly flutters its wings in one part of the world, it can eventually cause a hurricane in another. Your choices matter.

This Inspired Living choice isn't intended to make us paranoid about always being on our absolute best behavior. We're human! We harbor judgments. We step on each other's toes and values. We get to complain and fail. What matters is the underlying intention to be a source of positive energy as much as possible. This *is* your true nature.

Live up to the light
you have
and more will
be granted.

From a Quaker journal

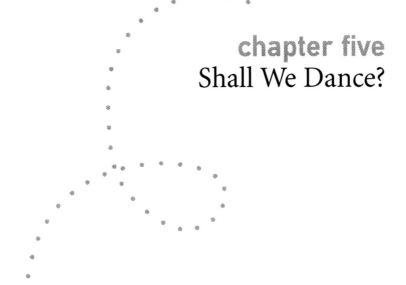

Shall We Dance?

Hope is learning
the melody of the future.
Faith is to dance to it.

Rubem Alves

Your New Dance Partners

Waking up inspired does not come from the things that you accumulate, where you live, your job title, eliminating all problems, having perfect life balance, or a hefty balance in your checkbook. Essentially, waking up inspired comes from how you choose to *dance* with your life. I mentioned that the second act of my life has a very different vibe. It's much more like dancing than climbing and striving. In this final chapter, I'll share with you some heartfelt parting gifts—essentials to continue your adventure in creating an inspired life. The following four dance partners and a set of four powerful questions will help you to keep dancing with your destiny in productive, rewarding ways.

Dance Partner One: Trusting That You Are Well Held

We have established that we are each responsible for creating our own abundant lives, and that everything is a choice. You have free will. We could also say that your true spirit has a sort of will or bidding for you. It wants the best for you. It wants to express *through* you. There is a beautiful and mysterious higher agenda at play. You can feel held by a loving universe that always intends to support your highest good. With each choice, you can either dance in sync with your true spirit or keep stepping on its toes.

Maxims like "There are no accidents" give me comfort and stimulate my curiosity about divine order. Feeling well held, I can lean into the wind or be willing to twirl out into the unknown, trusting something will hold me. Imagine that your first dance partner is this kind of trust.

As with dancing, at first, the steps feel unfamiliar and you don't know the music well. You stub your toes, fall down, get scared and want to give up. Then, you feel called back to the music. You choose to get back up and keep practicing, gaining proficiency and grace. You might even catch a glimpse of yourself in the mirror and feel, "Hey, I'm doing it!" Eventually, you surrender into the flow of the dance. The more you allow this natural rhythm to lead you, the more you'll discover a loving universe that delights in supporting you on your path. Over time, you'll experience an upward spiral of mastery and risk. Each choice reveals a new awareness, where you can accumulate both wisdom and a stronger sense of being aligned with your true spirit. Now, let's be clear that dancing with your destiny is not always serene and lovely. I think sometimes the dance is a bit raucous, not to mention confusing, and that's just the way it goes.

Dance Partner Two: Focusing on Inspiring Thoughts

If dancing with your destiny were taught in a dance class, the instructor might say, "Always lead with your belief foot." Operating as a creative chooser starts with choosing what you believe to be true. Beliefs set intentions. Intentions lead to breakthroughs.

How often do you end up dancing with doubt or letting your inner critic get you down? It's insulting to say, "Never feel doubt or fear." We need to have plenty of compassion for being human and not expect those aspects of human experience to just go away. So-called "negative" emotions are all part of the overall dance, and contribute to our sense of feeling alive. However, we get to choose the *thought energy* we engage and emphasize in this dance. You can proactively fuel creating more of what you do want by emphasizing more positive, hopeful energy.

Let's face it. Other less productive dance partners will still show up. Inner beasts will tempt us with fears, doubts and ego enticers—like uninvited party crashers. Your new choice will be to not let them fill your dance card. When the sabotaging thoughts croon, "May I have this dance?", you can bravely choose to let hopeful, inspiring thoughts take the lead.

Keep in mind that your thoughts create your reality. It's another one of those principles that's so simple and mind-boggling at once. What you focus on expands. If you focus on complaining about what you don't have, you'll experience more of that lack. As we have learned from physics, like attracts like. If you focus on your heart's desire, envisioning the best possible scenarios, you will attract the right opportunities and other elements to manifest that desire. Unfortunately, our culture often focuses on negativity and fear. You will need to make the choice over and over again to focus on positive possibilities. You may be statistically rare in your optimism. Stand tall in this choice. It will serve you well.

Dance Partner Three: Raising Your Vibration

All of the WUI tools are intended to raise your vibration overall - to have you feeling more inspired and alive. There are also times when it's highly useful to have the ability to change your vibration at any given moment. One morning, a friend's tragic news about a miscarriage hit me hard and started a spiral of downward energy. I had a new client appointment coming up in an hour and I knew I wanted to shift my energy to be fully there for him. In other words, I wanted to change my vibration. I allowed some tears to flow to release some of the heartache and then headed out for a brisk walk. The walking and fresh air helped to put a clamp on that downward spiral and redirect the energy to flow upward again. Back at home, I turned on some Earth, Wind & Fire music and boogied around my office, sensing the vibration lift in the cells of my body. I also grabbed an energizing snack. I was feeling dramatically "lighter" and in a much more solid place to serve the new client well. (The next day, I was able to process the sadness of my friend's loss and understand why it had hit me so hard. I felt like I had honored that energy, not just superficially danced it away.)

Another client, Vicky, came to a session feeling overwhelmed, frustrated with her team at work, and uncharacteristically cranky. My inclination was to play with raising her vibration rather than immediately talk about new solutions at work. So, we took a few deep breaths and walked around a bit. I then asked her to just tell me about things she loved or felt blessed about. She let the love flow, so to speak, and went on for a few minutes. Her menu of loves included things about her personal life, relationships, work achievements and personal qualities. She started to laugh and remarked, "Gee, I feel like the luckiest, most joyful woman right now. Wow." It was clear that her energy had shifted several notches up. Now we could tackle the challenge of how to deal with things at work with a cleaner energy, and come up with effective next steps.

I'm still exploring what raises my vibration and asking clients to do the same. So, play with what raises your vibration— music and dancing, showers, talking about your loves or passions, positive memories and whatever else you come up with. The physical acts of smiling or frowning will impact your emotional state. Different sounds can influence your mood. Phrases like "What would Jesus (or Buddha) do?" and "What does my heart tell me?" are vibration-raising catalysts. What's fascinating in all of this is how energy is evocable and malleable. Being able to manage your vibrational energy is not some warm, fuzzy idea. It could very well be essential for the clarity, focus and creativity you'd like to have available for your inspired life.

Dance Partner Four: Remembering Your True Source

Last but certainly not least, let's look at the illusion of dancing with security. Conventional logic and mass cultural norms still promote the path to the good life as jumping through hoops of achievement and securing higher paychecks. Reality TV shows make winners out of fortune hunters willing to exchange integrity and compassion for a million bucks and faux celebrity. You already know better. We are so conditioned to cling to money or the perception of sure-thing income and benefits for contentment. My favorite quote about this comes from Anne Morrow Lindbergh in her classic, *Gift from the Sea*:

Only in growth, reform and change,
paradoxically enough, is true security to be found.

We can still be enticed by the old cultural myth that we should go along with the standard program and hope for a decent retirement someday. Pragmatically speaking, economic trends actually reinforce the benefits of being more *inner-directed*. It's smarter to gain mastery in cooperating with your authentic destiny than to expect security from any external source. Stop and think for a moment about your true source of prosperity. Your prosperity lies in your ability to feel abundant. Ultimately, abundance is a perspective. Your prosperity is enhanced by your ability to attract and create experiences that fuel abundance. For this, you can rely on your inner guidance, your strengths and your creativity more than any employer or lottery ticket.

So, would you rather go for being inspired and self-responsible or settle for the illusion of being safe and sound? Your fourth dance partner is remembering that the true source of your prosperity lies within you as you co-create with your higher power. When you fully connect with that inner rhythm, and then follow through with your feet in the outer world, that is one extraordinary dance.

The Four Questions

Through years of talking with others about their goals, challenges and triumphs, a set of powerful questions has emerged. By asking yourself these four questions, you can revitalize purpose, joy and effectiveness in almost any endeavor. You've already answered number one in previous exercises. Now let's give you the rest of the set to help you continue to chart your course and enjoy the ride.

1) **What do you *most* want to fuel* as you move forward?**
   * Experience/create…feeling state, heart's desire/ vision or desired outcome

2) **What could possibly block* that?**
   * Get in the way/inhibit/distract from/disrupt/diminish…

3) What will contribute* to that?
    * Add to/enhance/promote/ fuel /optimal set up…

4) [So now,] what is the next best investment of your energy?
    • Be…
    • Think/ Reflect…
    • Ask…
    • Do…

My work with my client Leslie offers an example of how useful these four questions can be. Sometimes I'll use the four questions exactly as you see them in the list, and this leads to a breakthrough or inspired next step for someone. More often, the actual conversation has a more natural flow, yet the essence of the questions is there, as they were with Leslie on the day she declared her call to wake up inspired. Leslie came to her coaching call a bit sheepish for not getting to her homework with FAITH cards and "What if?" visioning. The week had been understandably crammed, and we encouraged her to not top it off with a dollop of guilt. When asked, "What do you want to celebrate?" she beamed with a new pledge. "It's time," she said convincingly. "I've made up my mind to make some changes."

Relevant to question one, what Leslie most wanted to fuel was "feeling more joyful and at peace." A key part of this was pursuing a new job, maybe even a significant career transition. When we explored what would get in the way, (question 2) her obstacles included kidding herself with that story of "When I get XYZ all done, *then* I'll pursue what I really want…." Like the rest of us who go through transitions, Leslie had been feeling plenty of resistance to change. She said that her inner critics were "freaking out about quitting her job or ever finding anything better."

On this call, you could tell that she had turned a corner. She shared that it felt like her inner guidance was saying that she didn't have to keep "proving herself," that she deserved a joyful life *now*. When I first met Leslie years ago, she was a single woman with a city address and a successful career. A key goal was to find and marry her soul mate. I've had the privilege of watching her walk down the aisle and create a new home with two beautiful children. The on-again, off-again desire for career change had been brewing a long-time for Leslie. Making that declaration to be in "go for it" mode was huge. I was so excited for her.

We then focused on what would contribute to her successfully creating her heart's desires (question 3) and how to effectively start this ball rolling. We looked at smart fuel with mind-body-spirit foundations, such as protein for breakfast and healthier energy snacks, instead of that mocha latte in the afternoon. We also agreed to dive into working with a "passion meets profit" matrix, having weekly sessions to help her deepen insights about her passions, gifts and fulfillment factors, and how to get paid for all of that in today's market. Perhaps the strongest influence for Leslie was tuning in to her Angel team. This was their message for her, written in her journal:

> *Leslie, this is your time! Claim it! There are many good jobs out there that will fit your passion. There is no need to fear. You are loved. You are worthy. You have earned your place in the world. And you have a divine birthright to a joyful life. Rise up! Transcend the mundane. Anything is possible. Look at how many dreams you have made come true (before). You are next in line for dedication and devotion. You deserve to feel fully alive. This will be your contribution to the world, to your family and to the flow of energy.*

Leslie then intuitively picked up on the next dance move, her own voice flowing in her writing:

> *My peace and joy will contribute peace and joy to the world. I will show my children how to live a peaceful, joyful life. I will do it now. My Angel team will support me! It is time for change. I am excited about change. This is the next phase of my life. I will be inspired… I will have a spring in my step.*

Although Leslie worried that this sounded trite, my heart sensed an exquisite breakthrough in her willingness to dance. For the final question concerning Leslie's best investment of energy, we wanted to find a concrete, not-too-big action commitment. She scheduled appointments in her calendar to start on her passion-meets-profit homework. We also agreed that she'd go to the grocery store to stock up on healthy fuel. When she grabs that bag of almonds, she'll know that she's also reaching for the life she deserves and is ready to claim.

Please take a breath and tune into your true spirit. What is it time for you to reach for?

Know that Leslie and I (and many others) are cheering you on from that place in our souls that is connected to you, our kindred sister. I already know that you are capable of living out the inspired life meant for you. And I urge you to…

> Be willing to really listen to your heart's desires, gut wisdom, and inner guidance.
>
> Be willing to have great expectations without being rigidly attached to a specific result or reward.
>
> Be willing to wait, or sometimes just to be still.
>
> Be willing to own the responsibility for creating your life.
>
> Be willing to have faith in abundant possibilities.
>
> Be willing to be lucky.
>
> Be willing to commit and make conscious trade-offs.
>
> Be willing to be inconvenienced.
>
> Be willing to let go of your ego's limitations and fears.

Be willing to unlearn what you think you know.

Be willing to love yourself more.

Be willing to invest whole-heartedly in this journey.

Be willing to wake up to who you are meant to be and do what you are here to do.

Be willing to enjoy the ride!

I once saw a sign in a deli that read, "Every person brings joy to this place. Some when entering and some when leaving." Choose to be a person who gives joy. Choose to receive joy. Delight in sharing your true gifts. Remember to keep refilling your own well. And keep showing up in your corner of the world, letting your true spirit express.

I wish you many blessings for the adventures of your inspired life.

APPENDIX

Wake Up Inspired Book: Suggested 13 Week Schedule

* Indicates most recommended exercise from that section.

WEEK	Read	Possible Exercises	Comments
1	Chapter One: Waking Up to a New Story	- Old Story/ New Story (Chart) - Hit the Pause Button: Take a Breath - 90th Birthday Party*	Select 1-2 exercises
2	Chapter Two: Having a Plan is Not the Answer	- Tune-In Time* - Reflect on Finding Your Joy	Select 1 exercise
3	Chapter Three (part 1): Three Layers of Inspired Living - Awareness, Responsibility, Choice - Values, Purpose, Vision	- Spy on Yourself - Reflect on Your Response-ability - Reflect on the Gift of Choice - Collect Clues about Your Values*	Select 1-2 exercises
4	Chapter Three (part 2): - The ING of Life - Mind-Body-Spirit Fuel	- Peek at Purpose* - Choosing Fluidity over Frustration - Hit the Pause Button: Take a Hike* - Tune In to Your Life Support Team	Select 1-2 exercises
5	Life Fitness Trail Station One: Hit the Pause Button	- Take Five: Morning Ritual* - Take Inventory*	Do inventory. Start morning ritual.
6	Station Two: Get Back in Your Body	- Awareness - Touch - Movement*	Select 1 exercise
7	Station Three: Explore U	- Play with Hats* - Feed a Passion	Select 1 exercise

WEEK	Read	Possible Exercises	Comments
8	Station Four: Make Room	- Play with Pruning Shears* - Out of the Closet - Break Free from Your Tethers - Reclaim Your Energy	Select 1 exercise
	Station Five: Assess Your Investments	- Check Your Balance - Read Your Meter* - Gratitude	
9	Station Six: Strengthen Your Spirit Connection	- Get Lost - Get Away*	Select 1 exercise
	Station Seven: Connect with Your Right Tribe	- Check Your Vibes (questions)* - Reflect and Recommit to Your Sisters	
10	Station Eight: Dive Deep, Reach Higher	- Trump Your Beast's Gripes with FAITH Cards	
11	Station Nine: Name and Claim Your Vision	- Reclaim the Success Meant for You - Connect with Feelings to Fuel - Vision* - Select Your Top Intentions	
12	Station Ten: Chart Your Course, Enjoy the Ride	- Your Compelling Charter - Creating Your Own Check In*	Create a Check In that works for you, for now.
	Chapter Five: Shall We Dance?		
13	Celebrate!	- See "Congratulations" at the end of the following 13-week template.	

If at first
you don't
succeed,
You're doing about average.

Leonard Louis Levenson

Your Wake Up Inspired
START-UP SCHEDULE

If you like, use this template to help you customize your Wake Up Inspired adventure. You will gain useful insights about what actually sticks and how to set yourself up to succeed moving forward. Copy and enlarge this image and add this to your WUI notebook.

Pace yourself. Don't bite off more than you can chew. Gradually build momentum. Celebrate your progress with each baby step. Accept falling off and starting up again without shame or blame. You're also entitled to change your mind on how to best serve your needs and real life. You want to make conscious choices, not let "life get in the way" as if it's running you versus you steering your own course. Remember the ING of your growth and progress. Use the "Actual/Comments" notes to genuinely raise your awareness about what's working and what's not working so well in real life application. Keep making adjustments as you learn what leads to sustainable habits and successful outcomes.

Target/Intention: Actual/Comments:

WEEK 1

Target/Intention: Actual/Comments:

WEEK 2

Target/Intention: Actual/Comments:

WEEK 3

WEEK 4

Target/Intention: Actual/Comments:

_____

_____

_____

_____

_____

WEEK5

Target/Intention: Actual/Comments:

_____

_____

_____

_____

_____

WEEK 6

Target/Intention: Actual/Comments:

_____

_____

_____

_____

_____

WEEK 7

Target/Intention: Actual/Comments:

_____

_____

_____

_____

_____

WEEK8

Target/Intention: Actual/Comments:

_____

_____

_____

_____

_____

WEEK 9

Target/Intention: Actual/Comments:

_____

_____

_____

_____

_____

	Target/Intention:	Actual/Comments:
WEEK 10		

	Target/Intention:	Actual/Comments:
WEEK11		

	Target/Intention:	Actual/Comments:
WEEK 12		

	Target/Intention:	Actual/Comments:
WEEK 13		

CONGRATULATIONS! It took courage, faith, self-love, resourcefulness, creativity and discipline to reach this point. Take a huge bow and celebrate! Your celebration could be shared with your coach or buddy/group. Take a moment to complete the following sentences in your WUI notebook.

I want to acknowledge myself for:

My Inner Champion chimes in with:

I am grateful for:

I am now aware of:

I deserve:

I choose:

Moving forward, I am committed to:

SUGGESTED READING & RESOURCES

Creating a New Story (Section 1):

The following books inspired me about possibilities for our *new story.*

- *The Breaking Point: How Female Midlife Crisis Is Transforming Today's Women* by Sue Shellenbarger (Henry Holt and Company, 2004)

- *The Naked Truth: A Working Woman's Manifesto on Business and What Really Matters* by Margaret Heffernan (Audio published by Penton Overseas, by arrangement with John Wiley & Sons, 2005)

- *Creating a World That Works for All* by Sharif Abdullah (Berrett-Koehler, 1999)

    I was definitely inspired by this author at a "Making a Difference" conference in 2004. I especially admired his passion for a Spirit–driven, inclusive approach to positive change with "expectant joy of what could be right" rather than anger about what's wrong.

- *A Whole New Mind; Moving from the Information Age to the Conceptual Age* by Daniel H. Pink (Riverhead Books, 2005)

    This is a fascinating book that's relevant to the "blending of both worlds,"(or both sides of your brain) and the increasing value of right brain skills in the business world. Also check out DanPink.com.

- *Creating Your Life Collage: Strategies for Solving the Work/Life Dilemma* by Kathy McDonald and Beth Sirull (Three Rivers Press, 2000)

- *When Money Isn't Enough: How Women Are Finding the Soul of Success* by Connie Glaser and Barbara Smalley (Warner Books, 1999)

- *The Meaning of Life* by Bradley Trevor Grieve (Andrews McMeel Publishing, 2002)

   This is a little, cute book with a huge, poignant message. It will make you laugh out loud and truly think about what you are doing with your life. Not bad for something you can digest in about ten minutes!

Your Inspired Life Fitness Trail (Section 2):

Station 1: Hit the Pause Button

- *Sabbath: Restoring the Sacred Rhythm of Rest and Delight* by Wayne Muller, (1999 Wayne Muller, Audio from SoundsTrue.com)

- *The Artist's Way: A Spiritual Path to Higher Creativity* by Julia Cameron with Mark Bryan, (G.P. Putnam's Sons, 1992)

   Consider Cameron's Morning Pages as a morning ritual tool (and other concepts) from this now classic program of unblocking your true creativity.

- *Time Off for Good Behavior: How Hardworking Women Can Take a Break and Change Their Lives* by Mary Lou Quinlan (Broadway Books, 2005)

For Morning Ritual Inspiration:

- *Daily Word.* Subscribe at *DailyWord.com* or call 1-800-248-6489.

- *Every Day is a Blessing: 365 Illuminations to Lift the Spirit* edited by Rev. Aaron Zerah (Warner Books, 2002)

- *Love Poems from God: Twelve Voices from the East and West* translated by Daniel Ladinsky (Penguin Compass, 2002)

  My copy is dog-eared and well-loved. Once, after teaching for 12 weeks, I took myself on a winter weekend retreat—a cozy B&B with a fireplace, a cup of black currant tea (or a glass of wine), and this book. Awesome gems in these pages!

- *Everyday Grace: Having Hope, Finding Forgiveness, Making Miracles* by Marianne Williamson (Riverhead Books, 2002)

- *Awakening Loving Kindness* by Pema Chodron (Shambala Pocket Classics, 1996)

  This is a tiny treasure, to pack in your pocket for nature hikes, or keep handy bedside, in the bathroom or by the breakfast table.

Guided Audio Meditations for Tune-In Time:

- *Invocation of the Angels* by Joan Z. Borysenko, Ph.D. (CD, Hay House, Inc. 2005)

- *Spiritual Power, Spiritual Practice: Energy Evaluation Meditations for Morning and Evening* by Caroline Myss, Ph.D. (1998, Caroline Myss, SoundsTrue.com)

Card Decks:

These cards could be a great way to Hit the Pause Button anytime, or to use as part of your morning ritual. You should be able to find these and other similar products at HayHouse.com.

- *Trust Your Vibes Oracle Cards* by Sonia Choquette (Hay House, 2004)

- *Inner Peace Cards* by Dr. Wayne W. Dyer (Hay House, 2001)

Station 2: Get Back in Your Body

- **The Institute of HeartMath,** HeartMath.org (for research information). Also see HeartMath.com for a more commercial site featuring performance-enhancing, stress-reduction products and services.

Books/ Audio books:

The following authors are leaders that first inspired me in the mid 90's. They continue to contribute provocative, practical advice for understanding and applying the body-mind-spirit connection for your overall healthy success.

- *Women's Bodies, Women's Wisdom* by Christiane Northrup, M.D. (Bantam Books, New Edition 2002)

- *Your Body is Your Subconscious Mind* by Candace Pert, Audio CD (Sounds True, 2004)

- *Reinventing Medicine: Beyond Mind-Body to a New Era of Healing* by Larry Dossey, M.D. (Harper Collins, 1999)

- *8 Weeks to Optimum Health* by Andrew Weil, M.D. (Alfred A. Knopf, 1997)

- *Anatomy of the Spirit: The Seven Stages of Power and Healing* by Caroline Myss, Ph.D. (Three Rivers Press, 1996)

    This is a great introduction to Caroline Myss' work and understanding chakras. You'll gain another fascinating perspective on interpreting your body's symptoms and signals to you.

Powerful and Fun Body Movement Resources:

• **DahnYoga.com**

Dahnhak is a holistic health program with ancient Korean roots that combines elements of yoga, tai chi and working with your vital Ki-energy.

• *TranceDance.com*

TranceDance is an amazing way to get out of your head, back into your body, and deepen your connection to that sense of Spirit within and all around you. Great music: *Shaman's Breath*, Professor Trance and the Energisers. You may also find this (and other music titles listed at the Trance Dance site) available on Amazon.com.

• *Nia-nia.com*

They say it's hard to define Nia—that it's more like chocolate, so you have to taste it. The website states, "Nia - Neuromuscular Integrative Action – is founded on the concept that there is a dancer, martial artist, and highly aware person within you. By melding various concepts together, Nia sets this person free." Try a taste and see for yourself.

Station 3: Explore U

• *A Hidden Wholeness: The Journey Toward an Undivided Life* by Parker J. Palmer (Jossey-Bass, 2004)

• *Crossing the Unknown Sea: Work as a Pilgrimage of Identity* by David Whyte (Riverhead Books, 2001)

Find the poem, "What to Remember When Waking" in this book, relevant to my assertion that "having a plan is not the answer." This poem takes my breath away every time I read it!

- *Claiming Your Place at the Fire: Living the Second Half of Your Life on Purpose* by Richard J. Leider and David A. Shapiro (Berrett-Koehler, 2004)

- *Love It, Don't Leave It: 26 Ways to Get What You Want at Work* by Beverly Kaye and Sharon Jordan-Evans (Berrett-Koehler, 2003)

    This book will inspire a practical application of "Awareness-Responsibility-Choice" relevant to your career, and stimulate ways to rejuvenate passion in your current work.

- *I Could Do Anything if Only I Knew What it Was* by Barbara Sher (Delacorte Press, 1994)

- *Callings: Finding and Following an Authentic Life* by Gregg Levoy (Harmony Books, New York, 1997)

- *Succulent, Wild Woman, Dancing with Your Wonder-Full Self* by Sark (Fireside, 1997)

- *The Woman Who Found Her Voice: A Tale of Transforming* by Susan O'Halloran and Susan Delattre (Innisfree Press, 1997)

Station 4: Make Room

- *Gift from the Sea* by Anne Morrow Lindbergh (Pantheon Books, New York, 1955, 1975)

- *Simplify Your Life: 100 Ways to Slow Down and Enjoy the Things That Really Matter* by Elaine St. James (Hyperion, 1994)

- *Take Time for Your Life* by Cheryl Richardson (Broadway Books, New York, 1998)

    This is especially useful for checklists to identify what may be a drain on you, plus encouragement about extreme self-care.

Station 5: Assess Your Investments

- **The Power of Full Engagement: Managing Energy, Not Time, is the Key to Performance Health and Happiness** by Jim Loehr and Tony Schwartz (Free Press, 2003)

- *Work a Four Hour Day: Achieving Business Efficiency on Your Own Terms* by Arthur K. Robertson and William Proctor (William Morrow and Company, Inc. 1994)

- *The Answer to How is Yes* by Peter Block (Berrett-Koehler, 2002)

Station 6: Strengthen Your Spirit Connection

- *I Will Not Die An Unlived Life: Reclaiming Passion and Purpose* by Dawna Markova (Conari Press, 2000)

  This is a beautiful example of one woman's journey, diving deeper within her own true spirit. It's also a rich guide for questions to ask yourself. Consider packing this one for your soul getaway retreat.

- *Spirit Allies: Meet Your Team from the Other Side* by Christopher Penczak (Weiser Books, 2002)

- *The Psychic Pathway: A Workbook for Reawakening the Voice of Your Soul* by Sonia Choquette, Ph.D. (Three Rivers Press, 1995).

  I am a huge fan of Sonia's work. While this may be a subject on the esoteric side for some, this book features clear, pragmatic how-to steps. It will help you clear blockages and build your connection to your true spirit.

- *Every Day Sacred: A Woman's Journey Home* by Sue Bender (Harper SanFrancisco, 1996)

  This is another beautiful journey with this author's self-discovery process and worth taking on a soul getaway trip.

- *The Alchemist: A Fable About Following Your Dream* by Paulo Coelho (Harper Perennial, 1998)

  If you prefer storytelling to help you connect with your destiny, you might pack this small treat for your getaway retreat and then treasure it in your library for years to come.

- **EdTownley.com**

  Reverend Ed Townley offers a lively exploration of metaphysical principles, sharing the basics of "New Thought" and Unity concepts. This may help you stir up fresh perspectives on spirituality, and expand beyond old stories that may limit your inspired connection to your true spirit. Check out the free daily messages and more.

Station 7: Connect with Your Right Tribe

- *Women Who Run with the Wolves: Myths and Stories of the Wild Woman Archetype* by Clarissa Pinkola Estes, Ph.D. (Ballantine Books, 1992)

  The Ugly Duckling story is especially pertinent to the Right Tribe station. This book is a must-have for the woman exploring coming alive and into her full expression.

- *Sacred Contracts: Awakening Your Divine Potential* by Caroline Myss (Harmony Books, 2001)

  The audio version (available through SoundsTrue.com) is a great overview about Myss' concept of having "soul agreement" relationships, and archetypal patterns.

- *Networlding: Building Relationships and Opportunities for Success* by Melissa Giovagnoli and Jocelyn Carter-Miller (Jossey-Bass, 2000)

- *Attracting Perfect Customers: The Power of Strategic Synchronicity* by Stacey Hall and Jan Brogniez (Berrett-Koehler, 2001)

  This is a fabulous combination of metaphysical attraction principles blended with strategic marketing applications.

Station 8: Dive Deeper, Reach Higher

- *Taming Your Gremlin: A Guide to Enjoying Yourself* by Richard D. Carson with illustrations by Novle Rogers (HarperCollins, Revised Edition, 2003)

  This small book carries a profound message for managing what Carson calls "the narrator in your head."

- *Law of Attraction: The Science of Attracting more of What You Want and Less of What You Don't* by Michael Losier (2003)

- *How Much Joy Can You Stand: How to Push Past Your Fears and Create Your Dreams* by Suzanne Falter-Barnes (Beyond Words, 1999)

  This is a slim book packed with ideas to inspire your creative process. Suzanne is a passionate advocate for helping people unleash their best. Also see HowMuchJoy.com.

Station 9: Name and Claim Your Vision

- *Your Heart's Desire: Instructions for Creating the Life You Really Want* by Sonia Choquette (Three Rivers Press, 1997)

  This is a great roadmap for setting intentions and doing your part to manifest your dreams.

- *Your Money or Your Life: Transforming Your Relationship with Money and Achieving Financial Independence* by Joe Dominguez and Vicki Robin (Penguin Books, 1992)

  I'm including this book for its relevance to reclaiming your definition of success. It will stir up healthy questions about how you choose to invest your life energy moving forward.

- *Imagine What America Could Be in the 21ˢᵗ Century: Visions of a Better Future from Leading American Thinkers* edited by Marianne Williamson (Daybreak, from Rodale Books, 2000)

  Let some of these big, sweeping visions inspire your bigger picture.

Station 10: Chart Your Course, Enjoy the Ride

- *Life Launch: A Passionate Guide to the Rest of Your Life* by Frederic M. Hudson and Pamela D. McLean. (The Hudson Institute Press, 1996, Revised Edition, 2000)

- *Wishcraft: How to Get What You Really Want* by Barbara Sher with Annie Gottlieb (Ballantine Books, 1979, New Edition 2003)

  This book has been around for awhile, *and* it still offers excellent tools for intentionally designing your life.

Shall We Dance? (Chapter Five)

- *Power Vs. Force: The Hidden Determinants of Human Behavior* by David R. Hawkins, M.D., Ph.D. (Hay House, 2002)

  This is a challenging and highly stimulating book relevant to "raising your vibration." This will take you to new depths in appreciating levels of consciousness (from shame to courage to joy and enlightenment) and the impact these levels have on you and the world.

- *Anyway: The Paradoxical Commandments: Finding Meaning in a Crazy World* by Kent M. Keith (Berkley Books, 2001)

  A poem was once circulating regarding a sign posted on Mother Teresa's wall. The poem included lines such as, "The good you do today will be forgotten tomorrow. Do good anyway." Kent Keith heard this story about Mother Teresa at a Rotary meeting, and was stunned to realize that these were his words, part of a student leadership booklet he had written thirty years earlier as a sophomore at Harvard! He was moved to learn that his words had made it all the way to India and to Mother Teresa's home for children. His words will inspire you too.

Stay Inspired: Options for Continued Growth and Learning

I hope this book has begun to equip you to create the inspired life you deserve to enjoy. Of course, a book can't fully replace the dynamic of coaching, empowerment group circles or all of the tools we use. If you're curious about continuing your own personal and professional growth, we'd love to offer support and resources tailored to your needs.

WakeUpInspired.com

Visit the vibrant community that we are creating at www.WakeUpInspired.com. You'll find motivating stories and free tools and resources to help you create your inspired life. As an example, learn 7 ways to enhance your healthy success with a free mind-body-spirit Fuel Check quiz. If livelihood is a relevant area for you, the Passion Meets Profit process includes several tools for uncovering insights about your values, passions, gifts, and purpose, and applying all of that for prosperity in your work and a sense being on your joyful mission. Scan our free e-letter, inspired book and music suggestions, and more. Peek in and see what appeals to you.

Wake Up Inspired Circles

Imagine a circle of accomplished, caring women working together with a passionate, certified coach to support you in creating your fulfilling life. You'll gain ideas, hope, encouragement and accountability support while applying tools in your own unique ways. Small groups meet virtually (phone conference meetings and online). Live groups and workshops are also available. For more information please visit www.WakeUpInspired.com.

One-on-One Coaching

Personal and professional coaching with Marian Baker is custom-tailored to each client. You receive ongoing support, with Marian serving as your champion, confidential sounding board, and brainstorm partner. We will fuel clarity, focus, renewed energy, and follow-through. And, have fun along the way. For further information, free tools, client stories and more, please visit www.MarianBaker.com or email Marian@MarianBaker.com.

"Working with Marian changed my life. She empowered me to claim the desires of my heart and to invest my power in a vision that has true meaning for me. Today, that vision is a reality I celebrate." – Theresa P.

Speaking and Group Programs

Keynotes, interactive workshops, follow-up coaching and consulting can be designed to serve the needs of your group or organization. Marian has inspired audiences on key topics such as how to fuel healthier success, blending mind-body-spirit vitality with real world achievement, 4 keys to creating the inspired life you're meant to lead, and "passion meets profit" for breakthroughs in productivity and enthusiasm in your work. Audience evaluations include, "Awesome speaker…Very inspirational…Best workshop we've ever had."

Please visit
www.WakeUpInspired.com for more information.

Please Send Us Your Stories

We'd love to learn how the concepts in this book have inspired you, and hear stories about new choices you are making. Any other constructive suggestions for improvements to future editions are also appreciated. Send your stories and comments to info@WakeUpInspired.com.

To Order Copies of this Book

To order copies of this book, including volume or special group discounts, please go to www.WakeUpInspired.com.

Other Coaching Resources

For general information about coaching, visit The International Coach Federation (ICF) website at www.coachfederation.org.

If you're interested in professional coaching training, also check out The Coaches Training Institute (CTI) at www.thecoaches.com. Books about coaching include:

Co-Active Coaching; New Skills for Coaching People Toward Success in Work and Life by Laura Whitworth, Henry Kimsey-House and Phil Sandahl (Davies-Black Publishing, 1998)
> This is an overview of the co-active coaching model and tools, coauthored by the founders of CTI.

The Art and Practice of Leadership Coaching: 50 Top Executive Coaches Reveal Their Secrets edited by Howard Morgan, Phil Harkin and Marshall Goldsmith (John Wiley & Sons, 2005)
> Marian is profiled in this book along with other consultants and bestselling authors. Aimed toward business, this best practices collection showcases a variety of coaching approaches and applications.

ABOUT THE AUTHOR

 Selected as one of 50 top coaches in America, master certified coach, author and speaker Marian Baker has coached and led workshops with hundreds of clients from corporate, small business, non-profit and personal growth communities since 1996. Clients value her holistic approach, blending mind-body-spirit principles with pragmatic tools and concrete actions.

Marian is profiled in the book, *The Art and Practice of Leadership Coaching; 50 Top Coaches Reveal Their Secrets.* Through her *Wake Up Inspired* book, groups and speaking, Marian is expanding her outreach in order to encourage and equip growth-seeking achievers to create the soul-fulfilling missions they are destined to enjoy.

Called "The Queen of Powerful Questions" by a leader of Coaches Training Institute, Marian has been quoted and featured in major media such as Health magazine and The Chicago Tribune. She has also been selected as an expert for Fitness Magazine's *You Can Do It* program. Marian is coauthor of the *Awakening Corporate Soul: High Performance, High Fulfillment* workbook.

Once upon a time, Marian's life appeared to be a smash success from the outside looking in. However, she gradually began asking, "Is this all there is?" and craving more meaningful fulfillment. Today, she's waking up inspired, humbled at the joy she feels in her own life, and delighted to help others fuel their own unique success stories. Marian loves this work, admires her clients, and will become your devoted champion. She falls asleep grateful each night with her husband and cats in Chicago.

Contact:

For more information, please visit:
www.WakeUpInspired.com and
www.MarianBaker.com

Email: Marian@MarianBaker.com

ACKNOWLEDGEMENTS

My editor once said, "Your husband must be a saint." She then started to apologize for how that might have sounded. I laughed and understood what she meant (imagining what it's like to be the husband of someone working on a book while managing a full-time coaching practice and several other aspects of life). So, my first and deepest gratitude goes to my beloved Kelly Mayo, for his understanding and support in many forms.

Huge thanks go to Terry Pfister, who did a stellar job of helping me through the editing process and became a midwife in the birthing of this book. Thank you for your loving care, professional excellence and delightful humor throughout so many hours, meetings, emails and phone calls. I am honored by your gift of sisterhood on this baby.

I would also like to thank several people whose incredible talent and generous, vivacious spirits made this book possible and the experience a fun adventure:

Jan King of eWomenPublishingNetwork for her confidence-building encouragement, practical support, and for shedding light on navigating the multi-faceted stages of book publishing.

Dan Paterno for being Dan the man of many talents, including the cover design and photography.

Nancy Cleary for the interior design, and for guidance through the book birthing process with her lively, fun energy.

Mary Dalton for her line editing and proofing with firm standards about the material, and for her friendly warmth toward me.

Sherry Hoesly and her associates for their efficient help with permissions clearance.

I would also like to extend thanks to Jeff Block, Stephanie Davies, Cindy Greenway, and Amy Kucharski for their contributions that helped me focus my efforts on the book.

I am grateful for my spiritual community at Unity in Chicago, which serves as a recharging base for my continued joyful mission. I'm also forever grateful for the teachers and authors that have inspired me through the years of my own "seeking and achieving"—too many to name or single out here. I am joyfully grateful to Coaches Training Institute and other pioneers of the coaching community. Thank you for taking the essence of wanting to help people create more fulfilling lives and shaping it into a distinct and distinguished profession. I am so in love with what I get to do for a living.

I am profoundly grateful to my clients. It is a privilege to share their vulnerability, courage, insights, triumphs, transformation, challenges, humor, and perseverance. Continuing to learn, teach and coach through what it takes to wake up inspired and fall asleep grateful is meaningful only through the work that we do together. This is a blessing to me every day.

INDEX